JELL-O

A BIOGRAPHY

JELL-O

A BIOGRAPHY

Carolyn Wyman

A Harvest Original HARCOURT, INC.

San Diego New York London

JELL-O and all derived terms are trademarks of Kraft Foods Holdings, Inc., a subsidiary
of Kraft Foods, Inc., and are used herein by permission. There is no financial or legal
association between Kraft Foods Holdings, Inc., or its parent company and the author or
publisher of this book.

Requests for permission to make copies of any part of the work should be mailed to the
following address: Permissions Department, Harcourt, Inc., 6277 Sea Harbor Drive,
Orlando, Florida 32887-6777.

www.HarcourtBooks.com

Library of Congress Cataloging-in-Publication Data
Wyman, Carolyn.
Jell-O: a biography/Carolyn Wyman—1st ed.
p. cm.
"A Harvest original."
ISBN 0-15-601123-9
1. Cookery (Gelatin) 2. Desserts. I. Title.
TX814.5.G4 W96 2001
664 .26—dc21   2001024739

Designed by Joy Chu
Text set in Mrs. Eaves Roman

Printed in the United States of America
First edition
J I H G F E D C B A

Permissions and credits appear on pages 145—46, which constitute a continuation of this copyright page.

In loving memory of Mémé,
the family's *first* gourmet

TABLE
OF
CONTENTS

Introduction

JELL-O *America's most famous Dessert*

COCA-COLA MAY SELL BETTER.
APPLE PIE MAY SEEM MORE TRADITIONAL.
BUT THE TRUE TWENTIETH-CENTURY AMERICAN FOOD
WAS CERTAINLY JELL-O GELATIN.

Jell-O was actually invented in 1897, four years before the twentieth century began, but in look and feel and convenience, it was way ahead of its time. Jell-O more closely resembles such high-tech marvels of the '50s and '60s as Cool Whip and Cheez Whiz than the Uneeda Biscuits and Gold Medal Flour that originally shared its shelf space. Jell-O was, in fact, one of America's first processed foods. As such it was a model for all the bland, sweet, cheap convenient foods we now eat.

The Jell-O business is also a paradigm for what has happened to American businesses in the last century (at least the successful ones), beginning as it did with one man and a wacky idea who sold out to a slightly larger and more established business, which in turn was sold to a company that became the nucleus of the great General Foods, which itself was later eaten up by the multinational Philip Morris corporation.

How American is Jell-O? So American that an anthropologist studying Asian immigration to Northern California noted Jell-O dishes among the Japanese *manju* and *mochi* at a community potluck as a sign of assimilation. In the early '20s, the Jell-O company courted new Americans with a cookbook illustrated by that arbiter of Americana, Norman

i x

Rockwell, printed in a number of different languages. Although probably less studied, the brand's selection of Jewish and African American comedians as its only two celebrity spokesmen nevertheless represents America at its melting pot best.

Astronaut Shannon Lucid did not have to cajole her Russian cosmonaut colleagues to eat the Jell-O she brought aboard Mir in 1996. They loved it instantly, presumably for many of the same reasons Americans do, but also for its novelty. Unlike Coca-Cola and Spam, Jell-O is rare outside America.

Is this because Jell-O displays so many elements of the American character? It is bright, brash, sweet, unsophisticated, lighthearted—even lightweight. It is democratic. There is no gourmet brand of flavored gelatin dessert the way there are premium brands of coffee, cookies, and beer. The Jell-O mold Bill Clinton ate at his first White House Thanksgiving was made from the same powder sold in Appalachia and on Chicago's South Side. It's also essentially the same product that helped convict the Rosenbergs during that famous '50s spy case.

If this is the first you've heard of these Jell-O appearances in American history, I'm not surprised. Because this is the first book about Jell-O that is not simply a compilation of recipes. Those recipes have been published in hundreds of Jell-O company publications and in thousands of church and community organization cookbooks. But before this complete biography, anyone curious about how Jell-O had achieved this popularity could do little more than gaze into their crystal Jell-O cubes. There was also no

How to Speak JELL-O

Jell-O is almost as popular a figure of speech as it is a food. The following chart matches up some of the most popular Jell-O similes and metaphors with their meanings. With its help you will be able to use Jell-O not only as salad or dessert but also to make up excuses, insult people, and even explain your shaky emotional state.

Like trying to nail Jell-O to a wall Difficult to impossible

Like trying to find bones in Jell-O Difficult to impossible

Like eating Jell-O with chopsticks Difficult to impossible

Like lassoing Jell-O Difficult to impossible.

Like guarding Jell-O Difficult to impossible

Set in Jell-O Nothing's really been decided

As soft, loose, shaky, or as stable as Jell-O Not very stable or certain

Legal Jell-O A slimy argument

A red Jell-O event An old-fashioned potluck

Feeling a little green Jell-O Sick

Jell-O for brains Stupid

As exciting as watching Jell-O set Not very exciting

Reduced to quivering Jell-O Nervous or excited

Knees have turned to Jell-O Nervous or excited

Reduced the audience to Jell-O performance Boffo, emotionally affecting performance

A Jell-O mold hairdo '50s-style piled on top of head

widely available history of Jell-O gelatin's invention and marketing schemes, and no explanation for how a product that was almost sold for thirty-five dollars in 1900 would two years later be producing a quarter million dollars in sales.

So how has a dessert that is essentially flavored and colored boiled animal skins not only survived but thrived for more than 100 years when more than 80 percent of new food products are gone within a year? Why is it served at every church potluck and most diners, hospitals, and school cafeterias? Why is it one of our favorite metaphors?

I will try to nail the Jell-O phenomena to the wall with three explanations.

One: Jell-O is pretty.

Two: Jell-O is the food that most resembles a toy. It's brightly colored, it moves, and, at least in its Jiggler form, it can be held, played with, and thrown. In a word, it's fun.

Three (most important): Jell-O is adaptable. Jell-O can be and has been molded into whatever people need it to be. This quality has been reflected in Jell-O advertising that sold it as pure simplicity after the Industrial Revolution and changing economic conditions left women without servants, as a food stretcher during World War II, and as "the light dessert" when tables were groaning with postwar prosperity and again during the '80s diet craze.

It's evident in the way Jell-O gelatin's role has changed from *the* medium of creative cooking expression when women were at home all day, to a fun way to spend some time with the kids now that both parents are working. It's apparent in recipes for Jell-O appetizers, desserts, snacks, and entrées. It's shown in the way Jell-O is used as a fund-raiser and social icebreaker; to teach science and make sculpture—even to style and dye hair.

These are admittedly some of its more unusual uses. Ask most people about Jell-O and what you will hear is about pelting cubes of it at a friend in school, about their mother making it for them when they were sick, about the "mystery" mold their aunt brought every Thanksgiving. They will tell you of eating it at showers and funerals. They will tell you of a food that is, I realized while working on this book, much more than something to eat.

Mémé's Strawberry JELL-O Pie

I first basked in the sweet steam of the magic pink powder while mixing up batches of strawberry Jell-O with my mom. We would pour it into parfait glasses and serve it with Reddi-wip. Later, she discovered recipes for Jell-O pineapple parfait pie and Crown Jewel Dessert, and I began making strawberry pie and Sunshine Salad Jell-O recipes out of my circa 1965 *Betty Crocker's New Boys and Girls Cookbook.* But my grandmother only made this one Jell-O dish. It was her attempt to replicate a restaurant glazed fresh strawberry pie that my mother loved.

1 ½ cups water

³/₄ cup sugar

2 tablespoons cornstarch

1 (3-ounce) package strawberry Jell-O gelatin

½ teaspoon lemon juice

1 quart fresh strawberries, sliced

1 fully baked 8- or 9-inch pie shell

Whipped cream or Cool Whip or Reddi-wip

Combine water, sugar, cornstarch, and Jell-O in a small saucepan, bring to a boil, and cook until thickened (about 10 minutes). Let cool 5 minutes, then stir in lemon juice. Place in refrigerator another 10 minutes. Place sliced strawberries in a bowl and add Jell-O mixture to taste. (I prefer a light glaze that only uses a quarter to a third of the Jell-O mixture.) Pour glazed fruit into pie shell. Top with whipped cream or Cool Whip or Reddi-wip. Serves 6 to 8.

NOTE: Jell-O glaze can also be made ahead and refrigerated, then reheated to a glaze consistency just before serving.

JELL-O

A Biography

Chapter 1

THE JELLING OF A LEGEND

*T*o understand the genius of Jell-O gelatin, you have to understand how gelatin desserts were originally made.

First you had to get two calves' feet—scald them, take off the hair, slit them in two, and extract the fat from between the claws. Then you had to boil them, remove the scum, and boil again for as long as six or seven hours—before straining, letting the product cool, skimming the fat, boiling once more, adding the shells and whites of five eggs (to pick up impurities), skimming again, and straining twice through a jelly bag that you will have had to make yourself (there being no Kmart). Then you would add flavoring, sugar, and spices; pour into a jelly mold; pack with ice; and go to bed while it set—it now being midnight. (Gelatin was also sometimes—no more easily—made from deer antlers or from the air bladders of sturgeon.)

No wonder that some of the earliest mentions of eating gelatin involve people like Richard II, Napoleon Bonaparte, and Maria de' Medici—people who were rich enough to have servants do all the nasty work.

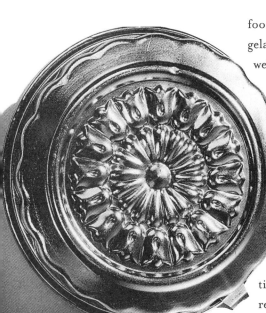

With the invention of jelly molds during the Victorian era, gelatin food making became high art. The little structures or shapes (as the gelatin foods were often referred to) reflected candlelight on the table as well as the Victorians' zeal for decoration and control (molds were, in fact, more or less culinary corsets). The Duke of Wellington's Apsley House reportedly had hundreds of molds, and almost as big a kitchen staff to regularly churn out gelatin dishes. Commoners only made them on special occasions or for gifts. Pollyanna handed out plates of it the way we hand out holiday fruitcakes. But she was famously optimistic. The author of 1877's *Practical Cooking* was more realistic.

"I have made calf's feet jelly twice, and never intend to make it again," Mary Henderson advised readers in the introduction to her gelatin recipe. "I would not have made it the second time except for the purpose of . . . getting a reliable receipt for this book. . . . It requires almost everything known in the cooking calendar; . . . do not attempt it with less . . ."

If ever there was a food calling out for a convenience product solution, it was gelatin.

Peter Cooper to the Rescue

The first person to seize on this opportunity was a man of many ideas. **Peter Cooper** invented America's first steam locomotive and a less successful gas-powered flying machine that blew up in his face and left him half blind. That did not stop him from helping to lay the first Atlantic cable, founding Cooper Union, and running the glue factory that funded his other ventures. Gelatin was a natural outgrowth of this business since gelatin is essentially purified glue. Cooper took out the first U.S. patent for a gelatin dessert in 1845. It described "a transparent concentrated or solidified jelly containing all the ingredients fitting it for table use . . . and requiring only the addition of a prescribed quantity of hot water to dissolve it." The accompanying recipe called for twelve hundred lemons, four hundred pounds of sugar, and eight hundred eggs along with allspice, cloves, cinnamon, and peach pits.

Cooper also invented a gelatin "eagle" to help time the gelatin-making process. Cooper biographer Edward Mack says its wings flared out or closed in accordance with the air's moisture level, thus indicating the best time to freeze the gelatin before drying. Turn-of-the-century boxes of Peter Cooper's "pulverized" or powdered gelatine boast of its "purity and honesty." Ads from the same time period called it the "cheapest and best." But it apparently never became as well known as Cooper's other schemes and inventions. If it had been, why would Philadelphia Cooking School teacher Sarah Tyson Rorer have felt the need to write a letter to the Knox Company of Johnstown, New York, in 1893 asking them to invent the very same product?

Knox, Cox (of Scotland), and other companies were already making other kinds of convenience gelatin products. But sheet and shredded gelatin still had to be soaked, and sometimes cooked and strained as well. So Knox hopped to it and a year later introduced "Sparkling Granulated Calves Foot Gelatine" together with a recipe booklet that explained the difference between food and carpentry supplies. "Gelatine should dissolve quickly; two to five minutes' soaking in cold water is long enough. Where it takes longer, it is more of a gluey nature, and should be used in cabinetwork only."

JELL-O's Father

The new product sold enough for word of its existence to travel two hundred miles across state to the home of **Pearle Wait**. As good as Knox granulated gelatine was, it was still only a food ingredient that smelled and tasted like nothing. Some additional ingredients were required to make it stand on its own as an appealing dessert, Wait realized. Although a carpenter by trade, he spent nights and weekends stirring up patent medicines, which taught him a thing or two about using flavors and colors to prettify a product. Why he decided to focus this knowledge on granulated gelatin, and exactly how he added the colors and flavors to make the first varieties—raspberry, lemon, orange, and strawberry—is not known (although it's easy to understand his interest in getting into the then rapidly expanding package food business). The reason **his wife, May**, called the new product Jell-O is also lost to history. Perhaps she didn't know gelatin started with a *g* or maybe she was referring to the way the product had to jell before it could be eaten. The *O*

sound was a popular ending for product names at the time, including Grain-O, a cereal-based coffee substitute that had made another LeRoy, New York, patent medicine maker a wealthy man. May may have hoped her husband would imitate Orator Woodward's success by mimicking the Grain-O name.

JELL-O's Stepfather

Orator Woodward started out no richer than Pearle Wait. Woodward's father was a carriage maker who peddled books door-to-door to bring in extra cash. After he died in the Civil War Woodward quit school to help support his family. The wife of the lawyer Orator tended horses for remembered him as being "full of ideas, energy, talk, brimming over at all times."

The first of these ideas he decided to pursue was unusual even by 1879 standards. "The business of the firm . . . is a peculiar one . . . and comparatively few even of our own people have an adequate idea of what is being done," began the *LeRoy Courier*'s

Woodward's cement nest eggs

article about Woodward's target

trap ball and nest egg inventions. The balls were predecessors to clay pigeons but darker than other marksman's targets then on the market and therefore easier to spot. The cement nest egg was infused with medicine that killed lice on chickens and provided the financial nest egg Woodward needed to expand into patent medicines. It was the patent medicines that made him rich enough to buy a new house and spend forty thousand dollars to turn it into a faux French château. He dubbed the house Hill-Bar, but his just-folks neighbors persisted in calling the "château's" two turrets silos.

Woodward's "château"

Woodward's first big food product success was Grain-O, which he purchased in 1896. The "healthy drink" was an instant hit in part because of the many evils then attributed to caffeine. "A strong man can live long

JELL-O
THE NEW AND POPULAR DESSERT.

We don't get any more whippings! Our mama makes
Jell-O for us and we don't have to get into
her jelly jars any more.

*Left: Wait's first (and possibly
only) Jell-O ad. Right: Jell-O
factory.*

and drink two bottles of wine a day. If he used the
same quantity of coffee for any length of time he
would become an imbecile or die of consumption,"
warned one Grain-O ad.

Woodward's advertising claims were at once more
outlandish and more honest than today's. The same ad
that began with the unequivocal and totally
unsupportable "You will live longer if you drink
Grain-O" also featured letters from several readers
who said they didn't like the product at first.

These ads apparently spoke to their readers,
because by 1897 Grain-O was enough of a hit to merit
a new factory building near the railroad tracks and the
formation of the Genesee Pure Food Company, so-
called to distance itself from questions then being
raised about the purity of America's new national food
supply.

At one point Woodward hired a relative to paint
this ad in huge letters on the roof and side of the
Grain-O building: DRINK GRAIN-O, TAKES THE PLACE
OF COFFEE. But when Woodward went to work a few
days later, his factory instead bore this message: DRINK
GIN, IT TAKES THE PLACE OF COFFEE. Whether this was

because the relative liked something stronger or
didn't like Grain-O or Woodward is not known. The
latter is certainly possible given Woodward's famed
cheapness. By this time he was pulling in nearly half a
million dollars in annual sales, yet his salesman still
traveled coach class and his wife Cora was not allowed
to buy expensive clothing.

Some of Woodward's money went to protect the
Grain-O trademark. The first legal threat came from
the makers of a competing product with the same
name but no hyphen. Then the Postum Company of
Battle Creek, Michigan, sued over Grain-O's package
seal, which they said looked too much like the one on
their cereal-based coffee substitute, Postum.
Woodward paid them five hundred dollars, changed
his seal, and thanked them for the free publicity
brought about by their suit. Later he paid twelve
thousand dollars to buy the Rye-O grain drink just to
put it out of business.

Some Jell-O historians think Woodward was also
trying to protect the uniqueness
of Grain-O's -O ending. The
Jell-O name certainly takes up a
good portion of the legal
agreement Pearle Wait signed in
September 1899 transferring the
rights to Jell-O to Woodward's
Genesee Pure Food Company.

*An actor dressed as an early Jell-O salesman
for the Genesee Pure Food Company.*

It's easier to understand why Wait wanted to unload Jell-O. Can you imagine going door-to-door and trying to sell this stuff?

"Yeah, I know it just looks like sugary dust right now but mix it up in hot water and put it into your icebox for a few hours and it will look like rubber and taste like fruit!"

Wait also tried an advertising pamphlet whose anticorporal punishment theme was way ahead of its time (at least judging from its failure to spur sales). It featured a drawing of a group of kids and this text: "We don't get any more whippings! Our mama makes Jell-O for us and we don't have to get into her jelly jars any more."

Beyond that, very little is known about how Wait sold (or did not sell) Jell-O although it's generally agreed that he lacked the resources to hire salesmen or push the product beyond the local area. Roger Lapp says Jell-O was just one of the many business schemes his grandfather tried and abandoned for lack of promise.

A Tale of Two Families: The Woodwards and the Waits

The Woodwards

Orator Woodward only got to enjoy the fruits of his Jell-O success for about three years. In 1905 he suffered the first in a series of strokes that led to his death in 1906. His will authorized a committee of three to carry on the work of the Genesee Pure Food Company. They were his wife, Cora, president; his eldest son, Ernest, vice president and treasurer; and his brother-in-law, Thomas Larkin, secretary. Among their first official acts of business was to acknowledge the end of company employment of twenty-two-year-old O. "Frank" Woodward Jr., a man who embodied the stereotype of the playboy son of the self-made man—at least if the tabloid newspaper reports are to be believed.

In 1927, those newspapers reported on how Frank Woodward had kidnapped his two children from his first wife, Persis Earle Davis, on the grounds that she was an unfit mother. He also accused her of having affairs with a dancer, a gigolo, and a Russian. Proceedings of Frank's divorce from his second wife, Mary Trask, were published in a 1940 edition of the *American Weekly* tabloid in a "he said, she said" format predictive of today's TV talk shows. She complained of desertion and occasions when he "crowned her in the head with a saucepan" and "threw a plate of creamed chicken in her face." He countered that she "wore dirty, shoddily made clothes and kept her boudoir in a

In any case, Wait didn't live up to his name and wait for Jell-O sales to pick up, and instead sold the whole Jell-O business to Orator Woodward for $450. That might not seem like much in a day when just buying the rights to air a thirty-second Jell-O commercial on television costs a minimum of $200,000, but it was a lot for a product that would not jell after being exposed to the freezing temperatures in unheated sales wagons.

Woodward sunk several thousand dollars into Jell-O to solve this problem. And still the storage section of the Jell-O plant remained stuffed with unsold cases. Coming upon these stacks one day while on a plant tour with his superintendent, A. S. Nico, Woodward impulsively offered to sell Nico all the cases, the recipe, and the trademark for just thirty-five dollars. Lucky for Woodward, Nico refused. For by 1902, Woodward had to double the size of his plant to keep up with demand for his now quarter-million-dollar Jell-O business. Although not yet "America's Favorite Dessert" of its hyperbolic early ads, Jell-O was well on its way.

---

nauseating condition smelling of clothes, dogs, old bones and food."

While neither settlement was publicly disclosed, *Genesee's Rich & Famous* author William F. Brown Jr. says Mary's claim that Frank spent thirty thousand dollars on his horses while she struggled to pay her rent convinced one judge to grant her the same amount in temporary alimony (based on the well-established legal principle that a wife is worth at least as much as her husband's horses).

Frank made big headlines for the last time in 1952, when he fell from the fifth floor of the Sheraton Hotel in Rochester. The death was labeled a suicide, although some family members contended he had simply misjudged the Sheraton's low windowsills while trying to get some air. (Frank was under twenty-four-hour nursing care for bronchial asthma at the time.)

The family's seams also showed on the matter of twenty shares of Genesee Pure Food Company stock Cora had been willed by Orator. In June 1911, Cora successfully sued her son and her brother-in-law to get this stock back. She remained on the board for what was undoubtedly a somewhat uncomfortable five more years or until 1916, when Ernest became president of the food company and his younger brother Donald took over the patent medicine business.

Donald lived in LeRoy his whole life and was almost as colorful as Frank. He is the Woodward LeRoyans most remember. The story of what Donald did the night his first wife, Florence, hid his car keys to keep him from driving drunk is legend in town. He called a local car dealer and ordered a new car to be delivered to his home immediately. That marriage ended about the time the finishing touches were being put on a new brick colonial manor house on East Main Road, so Donald had another mansion built for him to live in right across the street. Donald's third wife, Adelaide Jennings, headed one of the detective agencies that investigated the Lindbergh kidnapping. LeRoy Historical

Society director Lynne Belluscio says she's heard (a perhaps apocryphal story) that they met after Donald's first wife hired Jennings's agency to check up on his tomcatting.

Donald was also an aviation nut. He bought Amelia Earhart's *Friendship,* and made it the flagship of the private airport he built behind his first mansion. About sixty thousand people came to the airport's 1928 opening, bringing traffic to a standstill for hours. The first event at that day's air show was aerial golf, a game where pilots would drop a golf ball onto the landing field that a golfer on the ground would then try to sink. Subsequent air shows featured a stunt where pilots would land to eat a bowl of Jell-O and then quickly take off.

Other Woodwards influenced the town in quieter ways, giving money to virtually every public organization in town and establishing many that didn't already exist. Cora funded the municipal building and bought a pipe organ for the Methodist church. Ernest is credited with saving the town's banks during the depression, designing the post office, and funding a game refuge, a golf course, and the local American Legion headquarters.

The youngest daughter of Orator and Cora Woodward, Helen Woodward Rivas, founded a Buffalo, New York—based medical foundation for endocrine research that hired a mathematician who went on to win the 1985 Nobel Prize for chemistry. The foundation is now known as the Hauptman-Woodward Medical Research Institute in honor of Nobel winner Herbert Hauptman and Helen Woodward Rivas.

Rivas also donated $2 million to build the psychiatric wing at Rochester's Strong Memorial Hospital, known as the "R" wing in honor of her request that her full name not be on the building. Given some of the crazy things other family members did, it's easy to understand why.

Amelia Earhart, second from left, visiting LeRoy

The Waits

After selling the rights to Jell-O, Pearle Wait continued to build houses and pursue various side business schemes with little more success than he had with his gelatin invention. The Jell-O museum owns one pathetic letter his wife, May, wrote to her mother on May's forty-first birthday thanking her for "the dollar. I got my stockings. Guess you must have seen the holes in the ones I had." A few paragraphs later she says, "P.B. has been out every day looking for jobs but as yet found nothing." In fact, Pearle filed for bankruptcy only a couple of years before his 1915 death from complications of an appendectomy. After that May took in sewing and boarders to support herself and her two-year-old daughter, Dolly.

May's situation improved considerably when that daughter married the son of the founder of the other big business in town, Lapp Insulator, which makes insulators for high-tension wires. May lived with Dolly and son-in-law Rudolph Lapp until she died in 1956. Dolly's daughter Martha Lapp Tabone says her grandmother would occasionally mention that her grandfather invented Jell-O when the family was eating the dessert.

"Then she'd give a little laugh. That's all she would ever say about it. I think [Pearle's lack of success with] it embarrassed her," said Martha, a retired schoolteacher who still lives in LeRoy.

Nevertheless, May's three grandchildren have embraced this part of their family heritage. Martha, systems engineer Roger Lapp, and bank teller Susan Graney all rode in LeRoy's 1997 Jell-O Jubilee parade and decorate their homes with as many Jell-O collectibles as they can afford to buy on their modest incomes.

May Wait's Lime JELL-O Salad

This is the recipe for a Jell-O salad Roger Lapp says originates with his grandmother, Jell-O namer May Wait. He and his sister, Martha, both say they ate this "all the time." Like many kids, Martha Tabone and her siblings didn't like walnuts. "So we always picked them out and put them on the side of our plates."

1 large (6-ounce) package lime Jell-O gelatin
2 cups sliced red or purple grapes, halved
1/2 cup walnuts, chopped
Lettuce
1/2 cup mayonnaise

Prepare Jell-O according to package directions. Chill gelatin until slightly thickened. Fold in grapes and walnuts and pour into a 5-cup ring mold. Chill until firm. Unmold onto serving plate garnished with lettuce. Fill ring hole with mayonnaise. Serves 6 to 8.

Left: Martha Lapp Tabone, Pearle Wait's granddaughter, in her Jell-O decorated home

Right: The three Wait grandchildren in LeRoy's Jell-O Jubilee parade

The original typewritten contract transferring ownership of Jell-O from Pearle Wait to Orator Woodward's Genesee Pure Food Company is so badly faded that it's barely legible. But here's what it says.

Know all men by these present that I, P.B. Wait, of the Village of
LeRoy, County of Genesee and State of New York, for the consideration
of the sum of Four Hundred and Fifty Dollars ($450.00) to me paid by the
Genesee Pure Food Co., of LeRoy, N.Y.; the receipt whereof is hereby acknowledged have, and by these present, do give, grant and sell unto the said
Genesee Pure Food Co., its executors, administrators, and assigns, my exclusive
right in the manufacturing of the following named article; viz, Jell-O, to their use
forever; including all trade mark common law rights or claims I may have to the word
"Jell-O." I also agree to deliver to the said Genesee Pure Food Co. all stock and material on
hand, or that may be returned from any source, and all orders that may be received by me for
Jell-O on and after September 2, 1899, and to furnish said Genesee Pure Food Co. with a list of all
customers to whom I have ever sold Jell-O. I further agree not to enter into the manufacture or sale
of any preparation, that may be described or named with any word or words ending with
the hyphen O (-O).

And I, the said P.B. Wait, do hereby covenant and agree with the said Genesee Pure Food Co. that I am
the true and lawful owner of the said article and have full power to sell and dispose of the same.

Witness my hand and seal this 9th day of September, A.D. 1899.

Signed P.B. Wait;   L.S.

Sealed and delivered
in the presence of
Everett N. Bishop
Notary Public

Points of Interest on the LeRoy JELL-O Trail

Here are some LeRoy must-sees.

JELL-O Gallery, 23 East Main Street. Take the fund-raising "Jell-O Brick Road" (really a walkway of engraved-by-donation bricks) back from East Main to the stone building housing the LeRoy Historic Society's Jell-O exhibit (fully described in Chapter 7).

Wait Factory Marker, Lake Street. A LeRoy Historical Society marker designates the spot where Pearle Wait manufactured the first boxes of Jell-O.

D&R Depot Restaurant, 63 Lake Street. A restaurant housed in an old train depot located less than a quarter of a mile from Pearle Wait's Jell-O factory site. They serve Jell-O salad at lunch and have a tradition of constructing Jell-O sculpture for the town's annual summer Oatka Festival. During Jell-O's centennial year in 1997, they made a nine-foot-long, fifteen-car Jell-O train; a year later, it was a gelatin replica of their depot building.

JELL-O Factory, 57 North Street. The site of Jell-O's manufacture from just shortly after Orator Woodward bought the product from Pearle Wait in 1899 until latter-day owner General Foods moved out in 1964.

Machpelah Cemetery, 71 North Avenue. A few hundred feet north of the Jell-O factory is this cemetery containing the Woodward family's hard-to-miss mausoleum and the much more modest graves of Pearle and May Wait. Donald and Adelaide Woodward are nearby but not in the mausoleum, reportedly because they were Catholic.

27 East Main Street. Where Orator and Cora Woodward lived prior to his Grain-O and Jell-O successes.

93 West Main Street. The house where Pearle Wait supposedly mixed up the first batches of Jell-O, easily identified by the large, ornate *W* on the chimney.

THE LEROY HISTORICAL SOCIETY
THE JELL-O BRICK ROAD
DEDICATED JUNE 1, 1997

NEW YORK
FIRST JELL-O FACTORY
IN 1897, PEARLE BIXBY WAIT OF LEROY, INTRODUCED A GELATIN DESSERT THAT HIS WIFE, MAY, NAMED JELL-O. THE FIRST FOUR FLAVORS WERE STRAWBERRY, RASPBERRY, ORANGE AND LEMON. IN 1899, HE BEGAN PRODUCTION OF JELL-O IN A FACTORY BUILDING LOCATED NEAR THIS SITE. ON SEPTEMBER 9, 1899 HE SOLD THE RIGHTS TO JELL-O TO THE GENESEE PURE FOOD COMPANY OF LEROY FOR $450.
ERECTED BY THE LEROY HISTORICAL SOCIETY
DEDICATED 1997

Woodward Drive (at East Main). This appropriately named street runs through the former site of the Orator and later Ernest Woodward mansions and is now home to a dozen or more upscale homes. But the original stone walls, poplar trees, and Woodward family pet cemetery remain.

Woodward Memorial Library, 7 Wolcott Street. Orator and Cora's children donated the money for the town library as a memorial to their parents. An oil painting in the children's room depicts the escape of Jack (of "Jack and the Beanstalk" fame). Only in this picture, featured in a 1925 Jell-O ad, a crate of Jell-O takes the place of the golden harp. Inexplicably, the painting hangs under a huge sign that reads Cooperation.

Mercygrove, 7758 East Main Road. First nuns and now priests and brothers live in this brick Colonial Williamsburg–style hilltop mansion that Donald Woodward built and then turned over to the first of his three wives. The house once had a basement pool and laundry room complete with heated rods to dry the clothes. The grounds featured stables, a bird sanctuary, and children's "playhouses" equipped with electricity, plumbing, and phones.

Donald lived in a stone château he had built across the street at 131 East Main after he and Florence parted ways.

Donald Woodward Airport, Asbury Road. A hangar is all that's left of what was once called one of the best private airports in the world. Donald Woodward built it on land adjacent to his first East Main mansion and it became a mecca for visitors as did the nearby one thousand-seat restaurant-cum–indoor mini golf course he owned called The Barn (because it once had been one).

THE MEASURE OF A MAN ONCE WAS HIS MOLDS

Today we judge people's wealth by the make of their car and the size of their swimming pool. In Victorian times it was a person's jelly mold collection. The Duke of Wellington's kitchen at Apsley House had five hundred molds. Jelly molds fill a huge cabinet of Cornelius Vanderbilt's palatial summer "cottage," The Breakers, in Newport, Rhode Island.

The very best molds were made of copper but lined with tin to prevent poisoning. Each mold bore the owner's name so that the right molds came back when they were sent out for re-tinning—just as laundries today mark names inside their customers' dress shirts. Molds were also numbered according to the recipes they were used with. For the chefs at these great houses, these molds were analogous to a golfer's numbered irons.

The first and best molds were made in England. (Today these turn up on the collector's market for more than two hundred dollars each.) The democratization of the gelatin mold that occurred in America during the Victorian era spelled its downfall. The number of molds that needed to be sold in order to keep prices low limited the number and elaborateness of the designs, says David W. Miller in *Dining in America: 1850 to 1900*. The cheaper tin and steel materials used also made the molds harder to work with. If your gelatin dessert was a bear to get out and not very pretty when you did, why bother with it?

That, in part, is why gelatin is today usually served in glass dishes or, even worse, disposable plastic cups.

Chapter 2

SALES GET SHAKIN'

Even an official company history of Jell-O-brand gelatin admits that sales were slow in the beginning. To understand why, you have to think back to a time before ice-cream novelties and packaged cookies— back even before cake mixes.

While most turn-of-the-century housewives probably knew about the timesaving new crystallized gelatins from Knox and Cox, these gelatins were unflavored, and like every other one they had ever bought or prepared, had to be used in recipes with other ingredients.

Jell-O was different. It came already flavored and sweetened, and could be brought to life with only boiling water. It was, in fact, America's first packaged dessert mix.

Initial ads from the Genesee Pure Food Company placed in *Everybody's*, *Boston Cooking School Magazine*, and *Ladies' Home Journal* tried to explain this. "No baking! Simply add boiling water and set to cool," read a June 1902 ad in *Ladies' Home Journal* that cost Orator Woodward $336—almost as much as the entire Jell-O business.

"Works like magic," said another.

"No recipe book required for the new dessert," declared one that pictured a fashionably dressed woman tossing away such a book with one hand and firmly gripping a Jell-O box with the other.

Nevertheless, before 1903, the company had published the first of more than fifty recipe collections they would offer the public in twenty-five years. Early booklets included recipes for familiar and frothy Victorian snows, frappés, and whips as well as the more innovative Shredded Wheat Jell-O Apple Sandwich and Jell-O Marshmallow (made by dropping a quarter pound of whole marshmallows into partially set lemon Jell-O).

Shredded Wheat JELL-O Apple Sandwich

This 1902 Jell-O recipe contained a breakfast cereal and was called a sandwich and thus could be considered an early precursor to the Egg McMuffin. The original suggests having "your tinner . . . make the mould" but a modern 8 x 8 pan will probably do.

4 large apples

1/2 cup water

1/2 cup sugar

2 large shredded wheat biscuits

1 (3-ounce) package raspberry Jell-O gelatin

2 cups boiling water

Pare, core, and quarter the apples, place in saucepan with 1/2 cup water, and cook covered until tender. Mix in sugar and place in refrigerator to cool.

Dissolve Jell-O in the boiling water. Split the biscuits in half lengthwise, remove some of the inside shreds, and replace with the stewed apple. Replace their tops, then pour the Jell-O over them. Refrigerate until Jell-O is set. Serve with light cream. Serves 6 to 8.

Road Food

The booklets were distributed door-to-door by nattily dressed salesmen in spanking rigs drawn by dappled  gray horses (and by 1910, spiffy new motorcars). Working eastern, southern, midwestern, and, by 1919, West Coast sales routes in pairs (usually with the help of a couple of young assistants), the salesmen would place a recipe booklet under the door of every house in town and then visit the grocer to advise him of the impending demand. While this strategy usually worked, salesman Roy McPherson admitted to pangs of "conscience in selling to a small store what you know is more than they can easily use." Still, McPherson wrote to a family member who had once sold books door-to-door, "I think this work more honorable as the grocers can eat the goods if they can't sell it."

The salesmen were also charged with plastering the country with big canvas Jell-O signs, "a very sporting proposition as the farmers were never much in favor of the idea," Sid Ward once recalled of selling Jell-O in 1915. "We were shot at several times by outraged natives but only once with any effectiveness. The birdshot was removed from the salesman at the next town, and the operation charged

up as a veterinary fee. Repairs on horses were a legitimate expense—but not repairs on salesmen," Ward said.

Arrests for violating sales ordinances designed to protect local business were frequent enough that the company published *The Rights of Traveling Salesmen and Distributors*, a booklet in which one Attorney Andrew B. Gilfillan suggested employees assert their interstate commerce rights discussed in Articles 1 and 4 and Amendment 14 of the U.S. Constitution "in a courteous manner."

These same salesmen, and by 1915, women "demonstrators," would show up at church socials, banquets, and fairs to produce samples of Jell-O desserts and hand out promotional molds, spoons, and dishes.

Introducing the JELL-O Girl

By 1904, the company had a new ice-cream powder product and a new program of Jell-O gelatin advertising to supplement direct sales. Executives at the Dauchy Company, Genesee's New York City–based advertising agency, had decided that a child could best convey how much kids loved Jell-O and how easy it was to make (i.e., so easy, a child could do it).

The advertising artist assigned to the job reportedly considered hundreds of children as potential models before it dawned on him that his own blond-haired, blue-eyed four-year-old daughter Elizabeth might fit the bill. Franklin King drew some sketches of his

Good-bye!

JELL-O
RASPBERRY
PURE FRUIT FLAVOR

NO MATTER WHERE YOU LIVE YOU GET THIS PERFECT PACKAGE OF JELL-O AT ALL TIMES OF THE YEAR

daughter playing with some blocks that were summarily rejected. But the agency did like the photographs King had based his drawings on. The ad agency sent a crate of one hundred empty Jell-O cartons to the house to replace Elizabeth's blocks.

From that day on, the work of the Jell-O advertising account fell largely to Elizabeth's mother, Florence, who had to find clothes

and props for the pictures that were taken in the Kings' sunporch once a month.

"At one time I . . . made her little dress with ribbon bows on shoulder and sleeve overnight. And next morning, tired as I was, I had to find Elizabeth a new pair of shoes," Florence King recalled in a letter to her brother that was published in a 1940 edition of the *LeRoy Gazette News* newspaper. "Always it was an anxiety until the picture was finished. . . . Even with

the picture finished, anxiety only mounted until [it] was accepted."

Pictures of Elizabeth stacking Jell-O boxes, eating Jell-O, and preparing Jell-O (boiling water then not considered a danger to children) appeared in magazines and on store display materials until 1908, when Elizabeth was on the verge of losing her little girl cuteness. So Dauchy hired illustrator Rose O'Neill to render the Jell-O Girl forever young.

The Real JELL-O Girl Revealed

In the '30s, it was Jack Benny. Today, it's Bill Cosby. In earlier days, though, the person most people associated with Jell-O was a little girl named Gertrude Elizabeth King.

Elizabeth King didn't start out a star. She was just an ordinary little girl when her illustrator father decided she'd be the perfect model for some Jell-O ads he'd been assigned to draw. But twenty-eight years of appearing in Jell-O ads and recipe books and forty-one years on the box turned her into a phenomenon.

Little girls devoured stories of her travels around the world included in each package. Jell-O Girl dolls were sold or given away as premiums. The Jell-O Girl haircut became the rage. A 1940 newspaper article called her the Shirley Temple of her time.

The real Jell-O Girl was a grown woman by the time most of this happened. Elizabeth King's active participation with

the ads and payments for them stopped when she was only eight. Advertising copywriters and illustrators dreamed up all the rest.

So whatever happened to the real Elizabeth King?

After working as a secretary at Chase Bank in New York City, she married a Scotsman named George Muir whose job as a linen importer caused her to travel almost as much as the fictional Jell-O Girl. Their first child was born in Hong Kong. They lived in Shantou, China, for several years but left for England when the U.S. import business dried up during the depression. In 1940, she was living in a London suburb with her husband, son, and daughter and coping with wartime blackouts and food shortages, according to a letter she wrote to an uncle in the United States.

Elizabeth's daughter says her mother was "a very good cook," especially of

desserts and including gelatin, although she says her mother almost always served British brands that came in blocks. The exception is the one or two times just after the war when an aunt from the United States sent them Jell-O.

"I remember my mother pointing to the drawing of the little girl on the box and saying, 'That's me, you know.' And that's all there was to it. That's all she ever really said about it."

And so Elizabeth King died in England in 1982 amid countrymen who didn't know Jell-O or Elizabeth's important role in making it America's most famous dessert.

O'Neill stayed true to the eight-year-old's face and features, and kept the polka-dot dress that Elizabeth sometimes wore in pictures, though she gave her a neater hairdo, striped socks, and patent leather, colonial-buckle shoes. Variations of this picture appeared on most Jell-O ads for the next decade, and on the Jell-O box until the real Elizabeth King was almost fifty years old.

O'Neill also drew many of the ads—typically domestic vignettes featuring happy households with Jell-O. But at least one showed the flip side: two kids bawling into their baked apples because, the headline explained, "They wanted Jell-O."

JELL-O and the Kewpies

O'Neill is probably best known as the creator of the cupidlike Kewpie dolls. Although she did not create these for Jell-O, she did include them in a number of Jell-O ads as well as a 1915 recipe booklet that is now one of the most valuable Jell-O collectibles. The introduction to *Jell-O and the Kewpies* explains how "the beautiful and brilliant author of the Kewpies [will employ] her own cheery little imps, who are always doing something to lighten tasks and brighten the dull spots of life, to make the easy Jell-O way still plainer and easier."

The Crazy

Norman Rockwell and Maxfield Parrish are probably the most famous artists to illustrate Jell-O ads but Kewpie doll inventor Rose O'Neill is the eccentric illustrator most associated with the brand.

From 1912 to 1920, there was hardly a home in America that did not have one of her little nude babies standing on their mantel. World War I soldiers stuffed them in their pockets as good luck charms. People even brought Kewpies to papal blessings.

O'Neill once said the Kewpies came to her in a dream. Another time she said the topknotted little creatures were inspired by the turnips in her garden. The Kewpies debuted in illustrations for *Woman's Home Companion* in 1909 and soon appeared in drawings O'Neill did for many of her paying accounts, including Jell-O, although her financial fortune was made on the dolls.

"All the sculptors in the whole world from Phidias to Rodin never managed to earn collectively more than a tiny percentage of the amount she . . . extracted from that dimpled bonanza," O'Neill critic Alexander King once declared about her estimated $1.4 million Kewpie haul.

Lady Behind the Kewpies

O'Neill could have retired on the Kewpies if not for her frequent travel abroad and homes in Connecticut and Washington Square, Greenwich Village, that functioned as artistic salons for Kahlil Gibran, Edwin Arlington Robinson, Deems Taylor, and many other less famous writers and artists (some of whom came for an evening and stayed for years). Some say it was she and this scene that inspired the 1920 song "Rose of Washington Square" (although it later became widely associated with Fanny Brice).

The eleven-room Westport, Connecticut, mansion was heated by a giant steam boiler cast in the shape of a Kewpie doll, and was called Carabas after the castle in "Puss in Boots," in tribute to the many cats that prowled the halls with the artists. King said one poet who liked to work at the kitchen table frequently found eggs and marmalade on his manuscripts, and that a pair of shoes abandoned by a former Polish cleaning woman became the basis for a sculptor's proudest creation. O'Neill herself once admitted that she "never knew where all the guests slept."

One of O'Neill's biographers believes her increasing eccentricity reflected O'Neill's increasing desperation about the money her guests were spending as if there were would be no end to the Kewpie craze. Alexander King said a light switch that had broken shortly after O'Neill had taken possession of Carabas was not fixed for sixteen years. "The lights had remained on all those years, and they were still burning when I looked back on the house for the last time," he related.

O'Neill was, in fact, practically penniless when she died. But she has not been forgotten. Her Ozark Mountain retirement home, Bonniebrook, was restored by the eight-hundred-member Bonniebrook Historical Society. And the fifteen-hundred-member International Rose O'Neill Fan Club has sponsored archaeological digs on its grounds for Kewpie body parts. (And who can blame them when early bisque Kewpie dolls have sold for up to nine thousand dollars?) Members of both groups show up at the annual four-day convention held in nearby Branson, Missouri, called Kewpiesta.

The booklet shows the Kewpies helpfully frolicking through the preparation of eighteen Jell-O recipes.

Even when the subject was Kewpies or children, the object of the ads was to highlight women's desperate need for Jell-O.

"Keeping Trouble Out of the Kitchen" is the headline of a 1911 ad that shows a picture of a distressed woman pulling a smoky mess out of the oven.

"Cakes will 'fall,' pies will bake unevenly, and puddings will burn." But Jell-O "never burns. It doesn't have to be cooked. It never goes wrong . . ." read another O'Neill ad that wisely avoided the subject of unmolding.

Genesee proved they had hired the right illustrator in an artist's profile in a 1917 recipe book in which the globe-trotting O'Neill admitted that she hadn't "time to be a housewife and have never in my life made up anything eatable except Jell-O."

Savior of the Servantless

How did this Jell-O as savior-to-the-incompetent-housewife strategy play in Peoria?

Very well, actually. Millions of women were losing their servants to factories that were opening to make products like Jell-O. Before the Industrial Revolution, even middle-class women had help in the kitchen. Afterward, you had to be able to beat factory wages to retain servants. It's safe to say that many women were stepping into the kitchen alone for the first time. Certainly few of them would have had the time or skills to make their own gelatin.

"Jell-O democratized gelatin," says Lynne Belluscio, director of the historical society in Jell-O gelatin's hometown. One ad demonstrated this by showing side-by-side pictures of Jell-O "as like as two peas" being served by a butler and a housewife, the butler in one household and the housewife in another.

The 1922 recipe booklet *At Home Everywhere* sounded the same theme with pictures of a wealthy couple enjoying Jell-O on the patio of a Newport mansion and a Chinese cook serving it to cowboys on the prairie.

"Found in the most unpretentious homes of the old plantation [and yet] accepted by those at the 'Big House,' . . ." read the caption to a now racist-seeming picture of a barefoot black boy serving a lemon mold to a Southern matron.

Not surprisingly, the "Big House" Jell-O users got the most advertising ink. The so-called Dainty Dessert had long been displayed on fluted glassware, fine china, and silver trays. An elaborately bound and embossed 1923 Jell-O recipe booklet called *On the Menu* added the

I couldn't keep house without JELL-O

The Butler Serves and the Housewife Too

JELL-O

IMMIGRANTS' SHAKY FIRST TASTE OF AMERICAN CULTURE

It's hard to shake the memory of your first encounter with Jell-O as these excerpts from oral history interviews conducted by the staff of the Ellis Island Immigration Museum illustrate.

Recalled Paul Laric, who was detained at Ellis Island when he was fourteen: "Most of the people being from Europe and other parts . . . had never seen Jell-O before and when Jell-O was served for dessert hardly anyone touched it, not so much because they didn't like the taste but because they didn't like the . . . wobbly texture . . ."

Hilda Broksas first encountered Jell-O on the boat ride over from Germany.

"We were sitting there in this long . . . dining room with these massive tables and all the dishes tied to the table because of the ship moving. And they served Jell-O as a first course . . . It was a square piece of Jell-O and as the ship was moving the Jell-O was wiggling. And they told us we could eat this Jell-O. I was really frightened by this piece of orange Jell-O. To this day I don't have a great fondness for Jell-O."

Austrian native Rita Stanaland remembers Jell-O being served on her ship during a spell of bad weather. "Everybody was seasick. And I think one of the things I remember most, we would go in the dining room and I never had pudding or Jell-O before. Don't ask me why but there sitting was a glob . . . [of it] and the motors, of course there was a vibration on the ship and this thing is sitting there shimmying. I had a little tough time with that."

A Norman Rockwell illustration on a Jell-O recipe booklet in Yiddish

newly fashionable tea wagon and even gave the source for the silver and china depicted: "the most exclusive shop on The Avenue."

"Of course, anybody can make up fine desserts with Jell-O," sang out opera singer Ernestine Schumann-Heink in a celebrity series that also featured actress Ethel Barrymore.

Anybody and everybody, judging from the number of Jell-O recipe booklets distributed. The twelve million copies of O'Neill's 1915 *Jell-O and the Kewpies* booklet printed was enough to supply two-thirds of all American homes then in existence (and Jell-O printed as many as fifteen million of other booklets).

Some of the booklets were printed in French, German, Spanish, Swedish, and Yiddish, presumably to accommodate the unprecedented 10 million new citizens who entered the country between 1905 and 1915. In fact, Jell-O served to detainees or on boats was for many Ellis Island immigrants their literal first taste of the strange new American culture.

Darling of the Domestic Scientists

The transformation of the American table from a smorgasbord of johnnycakes, kielbasa, and lasagna to a common cuisine of convenience and fast foods was partly due to the wide affordability and availability of foods like Jell-O but also to the domestic science movement that sprung up around the turn of the twentieth century to help the servantless masses. The domestic scientists were trying to apply the principles of science and technology that were then transforming the outside world into the domestic sphere, thus bringing new efficiency and respectability to the home. They championed food that was dainty, easy to digest, and pretty (both for its own sake and as an aid to getting families to eat foods that were good for them)—all attributes Jell-O had been boasting about for at least a decade. In fact, the very box featured the words "Delicate—Delightful—Dainty." No wonder leaders of the movement signed on to testify to Jell-O's wonders.

". . . Even the woman who can not cook need have no difficulty in devising a new dessert every day if she is supplied with Jell-O and common sense," said efficient-looking efficiency housekeeping expert Marion Harland before offering some recipes for women who needed just a bit more help. Harland's Lemon Jell-O Whip with Prunes was billed as a recipe that would "take the prune out of its unpopular old place and put it where it belongs . . ." (overly optimistically, as it turned out).

Sarah Tyson Rorer of the Philadelphia Cooking School used her space in the *What Six Famous Cooks Say of Jell-O* booklet to rail against the heavy desserts that had been the nineteenth-century norm.

"Elaborate desserts, such as boiled and baked puddings and dyspepsia-producing pies, have given place to the more attractive and healthful desserts made from Jell-O," she said before switching into all uppercase letters for dramatic emphasis. "WHY SHOULD ANY WOMAN STAND FOR HOURS OVER A HOT FIRE, MIXING COMPOUNDS TO MAKE PEOPLE ILL, WHEN IN TWO MINUTES, WITH AN EXPENSE OF TEN CENTS, SHE CAN PRODUCE SUCH ATTRACTIVE, DELICIOUS DESSERTS?"

A later booklet featured Jell-O in motion studies narrated by Miss Farmer's School of Cookery principal Alice Bradley.

"Jell-O is an up-to-the-minute food designed to meet the needs of the modern housekeeper whose problem is to save time, energy, and money in doing her daily tasks. A glance at these pictures will show that few utensils and few motions are required to make either the plain Jell-O or an elaborate dessert," she concluded approvingly in her introduction to four sets of step-by-step pictures and extremely detailed recipe directions.

Although Fannie Farmer herself never appeared in a Jell-O ad, she probably did more to improve sales of the product than any of her domestic science colleagues. Farmer loved sweets and, by extension, sweetened gelatin. *Perfection Salad* author Laura Shapiro credits Farmer with the idea of substituting ginger ale for water in a gelatin dish, for instance. Farmer was also apparently a pioneer in Jell-O art, having once suggested that women pour wine jelly in a whiskey glass, then top it with whipped gelatin to suggest "a freshly drawn glass of beer."

Paradise Pudding

Adding fruits, nuts, marshmallows, and some kind of dairy product to Jell-O may not have become the rage until the '50s but the tradition dates way back to the 1912 Jell-O recipe book that featured this recipe for Paradise Pudding. Its name reflects its out-of-this-world, over-the-top extravagance.

1 (3-ounce) package lemon Jell-O gelatin

1 cup boiling water

1 cup whipped cream or Cool Whip

1/2 cup blanched sliced almonds

2 cups miniature marshmallows

1 (4-ounce) jar maraschino cherries, drained and chopped fine

6 macaroons, cut in small pieces

1/4 cup sugar

Dissolve Jell-O in boiling water and place in refrigerator until slightly thickened. Whip with an electric beater to the consistency of whipped cream. Fold in the real whipped cream and then all the other ingredients. Place in a large loaf pan lined with plastic wrap and chill until firm. Unmold, then slice. Serves 12.

Jell-O recipe booklets of the same era gave instructions for filling empty orange halves with orange Jell-O. Many recipes also called for whipping the gelatin (either alone or with cream and egg whites) and adding sugar to Jell-O's already plentiful supply.

Wartime Sweet

Such excess ended by World War I, when sugar shortages caused Jell-O to raise its price for the first time, and to advertise Jell-O as a dessert that does "not require [additional] sugar, cream or fats of any kind . . ." Jell-O now cost twenty-five cents for two packages or two and a half cents more than before but was still a bargain compared to high-priced fruit and many other desserts, Jell-O's 1920 recipe book *For Economy Use* argued, adding that whipped Jell-O could easily serve an extra three to six people.

The Genesee Pure Food Company apparently allowed itself to be duped into buying a series of now highly collectible

ads that appeared in *American Legion Weekly* (the precursor to today's

One of Herbert Stoops' American Legion ads

American Legion magazine) immediately following the war. The first pictured six ex-GIs in front of Jell-O packing crates—Jell-O company employees, the text explained, who had gone from tossing boxes of the Dainty Dessert to tossing hand grenades. The next *American Legion* Jell-O ad featured a Rose O'Neill drawing and a recipe book offer, which the *Legion*'s advertising manager discussed in a letter to readers in the same issue. He explained how the magazine was in trouble financially and that they were having particular trouble convincing food companies that women read the *Weekly*. A lot of requests for this recipe booklet could ensure Jell-O would renew its ad contract. Please write for it, he pleaded.

Veterans responded in such numbers that Genesee didn't just continue advertising, they also inaugurated a reader-advertising contest. The July 8, 1921, *American Legion Weekly* featured the winning drawing—a little boy poking his head out of his hiding place when the word Jell-O is mentioned—and the letter its creator wrote to thank Genesee and tell them she and her veteran husband would be using the two hundred dollars' prize money to buy a horse.

Genesee turned to professional Herbert Stoops for a 1922–23 series of *American Legion Weekly* Jell-O ads considered so outstanding that they were collected into a book given to American Legion chapters in 1924. The well-respected Stoops literally drew on both his artistic and military experiences (Stoops had been a first lieutenant in France during World War I) to produce somber black-and-white sketches of life behind the trenches—somber, in part, the accompanying text explained, because the World War I soldiers had no Jell-O.

A Jell-O ad by Guy Rowe

"The absence of mud, filth and general discomforts of the line, plus the presence of young and capable women who spoke English, were enough to make even the gloomiest and coldest of harsh stone [hospital] wards cheerful," read one that showed a one-legged soldier making his way across a ward on crutches. "What nurse did not wish that she could bring out a dainty dish of Jell-O to satisfy those dejected appetites . . . ?"

The JELL-O Gallery

Stoops was only one of dozens of famous artists who illustrated Jell-O ads during the '20s. Magazines were the primary forum for both advertising and entertainment in the country and the illustrators were well-paid celebrities. Most illustrated articles and ads for the same magazines—at the height of the so-called Golden Age of Illustration, it was often hard to tell the difference. Angus MacDonall's ads of a child being comforted after waking from a nightmare (of her Jell-O being stolen) and a grandmother serving Jell-O to her grandchild look like framed oil paintings with only the word Jell-O appearing on their plaques.

MacDonall's most famous Jell-O ad (also used on a recipe booklet) simply showed a portly man running toward train tracks to rescue a wooden crate of Jell-O

from an oncoming train. Almost a decade after it first ran, the company was still receiving requests for frameable copies.

Several other artists specialized in Jell-O still lifes. Linn Ball was known as the "Fried Egg Man" for some eggs he painted for a salad oil company but he also painted many beautiful Jell-O molds.

Nobody showed Jell-O's see-through quality like Guy Rowe (who signed his paintings Giro) and no Jell-O ad caused more controversy than the one Rowe created for the January 1923 *Harper's Bazaar*. Rowe had been asked to come up with something upscale specifically for *Harper's* but his depiction of two French women with cleavage showing shocked even its sophisticated readership.

An Angus MacDonall ad

A Maxfield Parrish ad

The most collectible Jell-O art was created by Maxfield Parrish and Norman Rockwell. Each drew two ads at the height of their individual popularity. Both of Parrish's feature the symmetrical poster style and the fairy-tale or nursery-rhyme themes for which he was famous.

Rockwell painted ads for well over one hundred products in his long career, including two for Jell-O. One looked like the artist's rendering of an early photograph of the Jell-O Girl. The other showed a grandmother preparing Jell-O with her grandchildren. They appeared in *Ladies' Home Journal*, *Woman's Home Companion*, and the *Saturday Evening Post*, and in subject and style were almost indistinguishable from the covers and article illustrations he did for these same magazines.

Gelatin Fairy Tales

Another important vehicle for Jell-O art were the tiny accordion folders that began showing up in Jell-O packages around 1908. Each monthly episode in the yearly series contained Jell-O recipes and preparation tips but also illustrated children's stories that girls collected as eagerly as boys would later collect baseball cards. In the nursery rhyme series, Mary, Mary, Quite Contrary grows "silver bells and cockle shells and rows of sweet Jell-O." And Humpty Dumpty "never did fall. He was too busy in watching the cook, making his Jell-O without any book."

In "The Real Reason for Rip Van Winkle's Long Absence," Rip was not delayed by sleep but by a group of gnomes who kept feeding him Jell-O. And the wolf would much rather eat Jell-O than little Red Riding Hood in the updated version of that tale.

But Jell-O wasn't shown or even mentioned in a series of folders that depicted the Jell-O Girl or Miss Jell-O (as she was also known) traipsing

Little Jack Corner sat in a corner
What can the reason be?
Indeed it's quite plain
He is hiding from Jane,
For a big dish of JELL-O has he

around the country and the world with her parrot. These were educational if Anglocentric.

"Tonio is my name and my father, he is Avito. We feesh. You go with?" a young Italian fisherboy asked the Jell-O Girl when she was in Sicily.

Another series of inserts showing Miss Jell-O in native dress was folded so when opened, her head appeared on a drawing of her holding a gelatin dessert.

The *Desserts of the World* recipe booklet covered similar far-flung ground for adults. Its discussion of Russian food favorites ends with a pitying, "Housewives and cooks there and elsewhere, who know nothing about Jell-O must often be at their wits' end when called upon to serve a dessert at a moment's notice."

JELL-O, The American Dessert.

This same booklet also makes a gallant attempt to link Jell-O eating with Eve's temptation in the Garden of Eden.

"Whether woman has always been privileged to prepare man's food for him or not, and to persuade him to eat, is a point on which history furnishes unsatisfactory information," reads copy accompanying a picture of Eve at the apple tree and glasses of Apple Snow Jell-O. "One thing is certain: for the woman who spends hours every day over a modern cook stove there are some delightful moments when she prepares . . . the simple, beautiful and delicious Jell-O dessert."

Sweet Success

In the '20s, Jell-O copywriters were literally recasting the world and world history in light of "the delicious dessert," and it was easy to understand why. Jell-O sales were booming. The company had long since dropped Grain-O and, by 1920, also sold off the patent medicine side of the business to one of Orator Woodward's sons. By 1923, in fact, Jell-O sales so dominated the business of the Genesee Pure Food Company that the company formally changed its name to the Jell-O Company.

In 1925, Jell-O's success caught the eye of its old rival Postum, then casting about for ways to expand its convenience food business. With Orator's widow recently deceased, the new generation of Woodwards agreed to sell Jell-O by an exchange of stock valued at $67 million.

It was not a bad twenty-six-year return on a $450 investment.

Wrestling the Competition

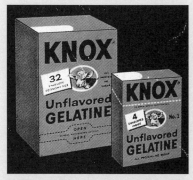

Jell-O was far from the only powdered gelatin sold in America in the early 1900s. Other brands, mostly of regional renown, included Chalmers, Minute, Peter Cooper's, Bromangelon, Peter Pan, Jell-Well, Jiffy-Jell, McKinley's, Plymouth Rock, Burnham's Hasty Jellycon, Jella, D-Zerta, Knox, and Cox, a Scottish import packaged in a red-and-black-checkered box.

Most of these companies sold unflavored gelatin. That included Jell-O's across-state neighbor, Knox. Initially Knox Gelatine was only a sidelight of Charles Knox's glove business (gloves and gelatin both being derived from animal hides). What little money he had to put into gelatin promotion he spent on male-oriented sponsorships such as racehorses and airships.

It was only after he died in 1908 and his wife, Rose, began advertising to women that Knox's gelatin business really began to solidify. A 1937 profile in *Time* magazine credited Rose, still in charge at eighty, for turning Knox into "a model . . . in both profits and employee relations."

One of Jell-O's few early flavored gelatin competitors was created by an ex-Jell-O salesman who once claimed to have discovered the Jell-O business for Orator Woodward. Although Jell-O scholars dispute this, there is no doubt that Otis Glidden left Genesee for Wisconsin and his own Jiffy-Jell gelatin company. Jiffy-Jell was distinguished by small glass vials of flavoring suspended in alcohol that accompanied the powdered gelatin. Unfortunately, the liquid Glidden substituted for the alcohol after the passage of Prohibition exploded on grocers' shelves. In 1921, Glidden sold what was left of his business to his former employer.

The other major brand of flavored gelatin made in America in the late 1800s was Dr. Price's Jelly Sugar Dessert (also known as Jella). It was actually only one of a number of food products that helped to make actor Vincent L. Price's grandfather, Vincent C. Price, a multimillionaire. The Chicago-based company's flagship was a baking powder Price created with the help of his medical school pharmacological training to make his mother's neighborhood-renowned biscuits rise more perfectly.

In 1890, Dr. Price sold his baking powder, flavoring extract, and gelatin businesses to Royal, Jell-O's only national branded gelatin competitor since 2000, when Philip Morris bought Nabisco and its Knox gelatine became part of the Kraft family of foods.

Chocolate JELL-O

Chocolate Jell-O is no longer sold but here's a way to blast to this part of Jell-O's past.

1 envelope (1 tablespoon) Knox or other unflavored gelatin
2 cups chocolate milk

Heat 1 3/4 cups of the chocolate milk in a saucepan (but do not boil). Meanwhile, in medium bowl, sprinkle unflavored gelatin over 1/4 cup of cold chocolate milk; let stand 1 minute. Add to saucepan with hot milk and stir until gelatin is completely dissolved, about 5 minutes. Pour into mold or dishes and chill 3 hours or until firm. Serves 4.

JELL-O Slogans

1902 America's best family dessert
1906 The dainty dessert
1909 The American dessert
1910 The fairy dessert
1911 America's most famous dessert

JELL-O Innovations

1906. Cherry and chocolate join the original strawberry, raspberry, orange, and lemon flavors. Cherry's still with us. Chocolate lasts an amazing twenty-one years.

1907. Sources disagree on the date but surely by the end of the first decade of the twentieth century consumers were able to buy peach-flavored Jell-O. By 1920, it was discontinued.

1918. Coffee-flavored Jell-O is introduced and sold briefly in certain markets.

1925. The first sugar-free Jell-O debuts as D-Zerta. The company gets the name from a recently acquired Rochester-based competitor. Also known as diabetic Jell-O, the dessert is made with saccharin and comes in lemon, raspberry, and orange flavors.

Chapter 3

JACK BENNY AND THE JELL-O PROGRAM

Postum's 1925 acquisition of the Jell-O Company was only the beginning of a buying spree that transformed the little Postum into the mighty General Foods. Following the purchase of Jell-O gelatin, Postum absorbed Swan's Down Cake Flour, Minute Tapioca, Franklin Baker's Coconut, Walter Baker's Chocolate, Log Cabin Syrup, and Maxwell House Coffee (despite years of Postum advertising preaching the evils of caffeine). After a chef on her yacht cooked her a delicious frozen goose, Postum heir Marjorie Post Hutton got the company to adopt Clarence Birdseye's General Foods frozen foods company and its name.

Initially, Jell-O gelatin also did well under its new ownership. By 1926, thanks in part to a price reduction (from ten cents a box to three for twenty-five cents), Jell-O sales soared from two to five million cases a year. But, as a 1934 *Fortune* magazine article about the company pointed out, "this success carried with it the seeds of its own defeat, for

Jack Benny and Mary Livingstone

it immediately began to stimulate heavy competition," from cheaper brands. Most significant was Sparkle, an A&P supermarket house brand that cost only five cents and was 1.5 ounces bigger than Jell-O.

This being the depression, value was a big issue with consumers, so Jell-O lowered its price to match Sparkle. As a result, by 1933, Jell-O was only earning a third of what it had in 1924.

Radio to the Rescue

For help General Foods turned to Young & Rubicam, a fledgling ad agency that had done wonders for Postum. The agency decided to make Jell-O part of an early experiment in radio advertising called "The Cooking School of the Air," consisting of fifteen minutes of ads and demonstrations of General Foods products. The program was hosted by General Foods' version of Betty Crocker, Frances Lee Barton (really a mother of eight named Isabella Beach). *Fortune* said Mrs. Barton brought

"messages of hope and cheer to the American housewife at 10:15 on Tuesday and Thursday mornings, together with recipes for cakes, puddings, and whatnot." By 1934, "Mrs. Barton" was sending out weekly recipe bulletins to some fifty-two hundred paying subscribers and personally answering two thousand letters a week of the "cake blew up" variety.

An illustration from Frances Lee Barton's class book

In 1933, Jell-O also started its own thrice-weekly, fifteen-minute show based on L. Frank Baum's *Wizard of Oz* books. To help promote the show, four of the six *Little Wizard* Oz books were reprinted and offered to listeners who sent in a dime plus Jell-O box tops. The books were identical to the original 1913 versions except for a back-cover picture of the Scarecrow and the Tin Man carrying a gelatin mold and an advertising insert that did its best to link Jell-O with the stories.

"Surely a wizard invented Jell-O desserts!" began one advertising page from *Tiktok and the Nome King*. "Magic! Right in Mother's kitchen! Jell-O desserts seem like something right out of Oz!" read the inside cover of *The Scarecrow and the Tin Wood-Man*, a booklet that also offered recipes for Emerald Fruit Cup (made with lime Jell-O) and Junior Sailboats (peaches shaped like boats stuck with toothpick masts floating on a sea of orange or lemon Jell-O).

Nevertheless, "Jell-O was in deep trouble," Lou Brockway, the account supervisor for General Foods at Young & Rubicam, later recalled. "The major reason was that Royal Gelatin tasted better than Jell-O."

So General Foods introduced a "New Jell-O" with "locked-in" flavor. If the ads could be believed, it set faster, was more tender, and, most importantly, tasted better because, as one ad explained, "all the fruit flavor, tart and juicy-fresh, is right there, imprisoned in the tender, shining Jell-O. None of it has been carried away on clouds of useless steam." (There was

no steam because New Jell-O was made without boiling water.)

Jell-O ads invited women to prove it for themselves by smelling Jell-O (both before and after mixing it with warm water), and its competitors followed suit. In fact, it's hard to find a women's magazine from 1934 or 1935 that does not contain an ad of a woman with a Royal, Knox, or Jell-O gelatin box up her nose.

O-o-o! *What a Smell!*

Taking a Chance on Benny

Not everyone was impressed with the New Jell-O. It did not help that "Royal was using radio with a show featuring Fanny Brice," said Young & Rubicam's Brockway. Young & Rubicam decided Jell-O also needed to sponsor a high-profile radio show. They settled on Jack Benny, who had gone through three sponsors in two years making fun of their products.

"We were very frank with our client in presenting Benny," said Brockway. "We said he was not our first or second or third choice, but he was available and he had a good, if not outstanding record . . .

"The time, 7 P.M. Sunday night, was another gamble. That and 10 P.M. Friday night were the only two times available. We wanted to reach kids so we took the Sunday 7 P.M. time, in spite of the fact that no show had ever been successful at that time."

Jack Benny himself viewed his hiring as an act of desperation. Jell-O "came in six delicious flavors, all of them totally ignored by the consumers. From coast to coast, stores were stocked with mountains of unsold Jell-O. The board of directors considered scrapping the entire product, but as a last-ditch stand, they hired me," wrote Benny in his memoir, *Sunday Nights at Seven.*

So Benny, hired because he was practically the only comic available, went on the air in a dubious time slot

the first Sunday in October 1934—and was a huge hit. Every week more and more people tuned in to hear Benny spoof the latest movie and banter with his portly announcer, naive singer, playboy bandleader, and sharp-tongued wife.

Unfortunately, Jell-O sales did not grow as fast as the show's listenership. "October passed by with no

The Jell-O program cast, starring Jack Benny

Jack, Don, and Mary reading. Standing: George Balzar, the writer. Lower right: Ollie O'Toole, an actor.

A Sponsorship Congeals

For the next eight years as many as 40 million Americans settled down on Sunday night to hear Benny's "Jell-O again" greeting, the five-note ascending "J-E-L-L [pause] O" jingle, and Don Wilson go on about the "six delicious flavors" now "locked in by a new, exclusive process" that made them even "richer, grander, and more tempting"—not to mention the "brilliant, gay colors" also found only in the box with "the big red letters."

discernible results. Likewise November . . . During the last week in December the product manager told me that Benny would not be continued after his twenty weeks," said Brockway.

In her memoir, *Jack Benny*, Benny's wife and costar, Mary Livingstone, recalled how the couple's agent showed up in their apartment one day to say the sponsor wanted to cut cast salaries across the board. Instead Benny and Livingstone said they would work for free if the other salaries could remain untouched. The gamble paid off. Jell-O sales picked up. By the first week of January 1935, they were the highest for any week since General Foods had owned the business. To celebrate, General Foods held a party at which the Bennys were presented with a check for their forfeited salaries and an ornately decorated six-tier Jell-O mold.

The Benny show is frequently praised for its funny commercials. In fact, the ads themselves were fairly straight. It was their hyperbolic language and announcer Wilson's enthusiastic delivery that created the comic opportunity for Benny to refer to Wilson's "wiggly waist" or "six delicious flavors' sway," for instance. Wilson, in turn, introduced Benny as "that shimmering, quivering, ice-kissed comedian."

Jell-O also often got worked into the show skits. When Benny bragged about having to walk to school through ten miles of snow in one winter 1937 episode, Wilson retorted that he had to "eat through ten miles of Jell-O." In a March 1937 program most notable for marking Eddie Anderson's first appearance on the show (as a train porter rather than as Rochester), zany train announcements included the recitation of Jell-O's strawberry, raspberry, cherry, orange, lemon, and lime flavors. Mary, whose poems were infamous, recited this one on Jack's 1939 birthday show: "Oh, Jack Benny, oh Jack Benny / You've had birthdays, but how many?/ So happy returns, and all good wishes/ From us and Jell-O, So delicious."

In the show's parody of the 1937 film *Wife, Doctor, and Nurse* Don Wilson plays a patient whose symptom is reciting the six flavors of Jell-O. "Dr." Benny asks if he's also still seeing "those big red letters on the box."

The introduction to Benny's January 1935 spoof of the French classic *The Count of Monte Cristo*, called "The Count of Monte Jell-O," explained that hero Edmond Dantes (played by French actor *Jacques* Benny) had been placed in a dungeon for fourteen years with the same sponsor after being wrongly accused of spying.

The scene opens with Benny in the dungeon.

"The silence is driving me mad! Talk to me, somebody. Say something!"

Don Wilson

"Jell-O has that new extra rich fruit flavor," Don Wilson's voice booms out in reply. "It tastes twice as

good as ever before and you can get it in all six delicious flavors."

"Is there no end to this torture?" Benny screams.

Later Benny escapes the dungeon and travels to the island with the buried treasure—boxes of Jell-O, of course.

Jack and Mary were also featured in Jell-O print ads and a 1937 recipe book. The print ads were in a

Sunday funnies format. In one, Mary helps a hillbilly girl who "cain't cook nohow" charm some feudin' families by showing her how to make Jell-O.

"Ye musta witched it! A while ago it was like water an' now it stands up proud like yon mountain!" the amazed girl says after watching Mary unmold a batch.

Jack & Mary's Recipe Book, which went through three printings, featured cartoon and photo composites of Jack and Mary spouting commercials disguised as corny riddles such as:

Why is Jell-O like a man with his chair pulled out from under him?
Because it sets faster.

Why is Jell-O like a woman taking a package of raisins to Europe?
It makes a little fruit go such a long way!

Rochester as Revolutionary

African American actor Eddie Anderson first appeared on *The Jack Benny Program* in 1937 as a train porter who had never heard of Albuquerque. This guest appearance was such a hit that he was soon brought back to play the permanent role of Benny's valet, Rochester Van Jones.

Being the person who drove Benny's dilapidated Maxwell automobile, laid out his moth-eaten suits, and prepared the meager offerings at Benny's dinner parties gave Rochester the ammunition to needle his boss and produce some of the show's biggest laughs.

And yet, Rochester's early appearances were marred by the character's subservient manner and stereotypic references to his fondness for gambling, liquor, and the ladies. Anderson's guest appearances were never publicized on the show as they were for other cast members. And he wasn't mentioned in the show's opening credits until 1941.

In 1965, the revolutionary black theater figure LeRoi Jones, now known as Amiri Baraka, addressed these injustices with a one-act play that placed a Rochester with an Afro and the attitude of a black militant in the otherwise familiar Benny show format.

The play, *Jello*, opens with Rochester flatly refusing to bring around Benny's car. When Benny tries to reason with him, in part by addressing him as "friend" (and, even worse, "my chocolate friend"), Rochester challenges that as well.

"If we so tight, why're you the one with all the money, and I work for you? That don't sound like friend to me. That just like a natural slave . . . ," Jones's Rochester said.

The real "Jell-O Program" got a lot of comic mileage out of the idea that Benny was rich because he penny-pinched. But *Jello* suggested darker reasons.

"What you own, one of them appliance stores on 125th Street?" Rochester asks him at one point. "You own a few butcher stores and stuff too.

Prices ten cents higher than downtown too."

"Look, I'm not there, I don't control the policies. I'm a comedian, an artist," Benny protests in reply.

To redress the imbalance, Rochester holds Benny up. Other cast members who enter think the robbery is part of one of the show's skits and do nothing to stop it. Mary Livingstone's main concern is how the sponsor will react to dialogue that was "not in the approved script" until Rochester robs her too and she faints. Last to go down is announcer Don Wilson, who delivers a Jell-O commercial amid the unconscious bodies of the other cast members.

Going through Wilson's clothes for money, Rochester finds only Jell-O boxes until, Jones's stage directions note, he "Finally finds money bag, tied in Jell-O bag." The play ends with Rochester getting both the money and his wish to get driven for a change—in a getaway car.

The play was a big hit with audiences

of the Black Arts Repertory Theatre/School in Harlem where it was first performed.

While not considered to be on the level of complexity of *Dutchman* or *The Toilet*, two other plays Jones wrote about the same time, critics saw it as an effective "inversion of white popular images of blacks."

In the critical work *Amiri Baraka*, Lloyd W. Brown says the trouble the Benny show cast members have in distinguishing between the show and real life in *Jello* reflects the unrealistic ideas the white world has about blacks. ". . . such fantasies make it difficult for whites to recognize the validity of militant claims when blacks do break away from the docile stereotype," Brown writes. Jones's faithfulness to the original Benny show format also allows him to make "convincing links" between the old and new Rochesters. "Despite his compliance the original Rochester is sufficiently saucy in his relationship with Jack Benny to suggest a certain predisposition toward rebelliousness," Brown says.

But the tough tone and language of *Jello* was apparently too much for publisher Bobbs-Merrill, who refused to publish it in Jones's 1969 collection, *Four Black Revolutionary Plays*. Third World Press came to the rescue the next year, publishing *Jello* with an introduction, also written by Jones, entitled "Negro Theater Pimps Get Big Off Nationalism."

The puns in the cartoon centerfold depicting Jack and Mary's visit to the General Foods kitchens were even worse.

"I've always wanted to know how to whip Jell-O," Mary tells a kitchens' employee in a panel featuring a recipe for prune whip as Jack looks on.

"Just chill your dissolved Jell-O until it's syrupy—then put it in a bowl of cracked ice, and beat it!" the worker patiently explains.

"Beat it? What have we done to get kicked out so soon?" Benny wonders.

Benny *did* get kicked out of the Jell-O business—although it wasn't until 1942. War-related sugar shortages sharply reduced production and made it easy for the company to sell every box of Jell-O without Benny's help. So General Foods decided to change Benny's sponsorship to something in more plentiful supply.

The switch became the subject of one of Benny's last shows for Jell-O. In it, Benny is summoned to a meeting with General Foods' board chair Charles Mortimer that Benny fears will be about his show's cancellation.

"Jell-O needs you," Don Wilson tells Jack reassuringly.

"I'd feel a lot better if I was sliced bananas," Benny replies.

Two years later Benny and General Foods parted ways entirely. Although there was no official explanation, the show's ratings had dropped during the war and the show was expensive (Benny alone got $600,000 in 1940 and the show ate up three-quarters of Jell-O's advertising budget). In the memoirs he cowrote with his daughter, Benny said, "The American Tobacco Company made me a handsome offer, which General Foods did not match."

Whatever the case, Benny's first show for Lucky Strike included a moment when Benny reminded announcer Don Wilson that Luckies didn't come in six delicious flavors.

The Jell-O references would continue throughout Benny's career—probably because they continued to get laughs. They included a 1951 medical sketch where a doctor looks at Jack's X ray and sees strawberry, raspberry, cherry, orange, lemon, and lime ("Haven't you eaten since then?" he asks) and a 1955 carnival bit where a strong man grabs Benny's arm and wonders, "Is that your muscle or are you still plugging Jell-O?"

Officially Benny only plugged Jell-O once more—on his television show during the 1962–63 season. During the course of his career Benny sold Lucky Strikes for almost twice as long as Jell-O.

Nevertheless, former Benny show writer Milt Josefsberg reports that when middle-aged Americans were asked in 1973 to name Jack Benny's radio sponsor, 40 percent of them said Jell-O.

This despite the fact that Mary Livingstone said Benny "never ate" the stuff.

4½ OZ.   127 GMS.

SUGAR · DEXTROSE · CORNSTARCH · WHEAT STARCH · WHEAT FLOUR · COCOA · SALT · FLAVORING · U·S·CERTIFIED COLOR

REG. U. S. PAT. OFF.

JELL-O
CHOCOLATE
FLAVOR
PUDDING

JUST ADD MiLK

MANUFACTURED IN U.S.A. BY GENERAL FOODS CORPORATION, ADDRESS: NEW YORK, N.Y.

"A hit with men? You bet!" says Kate Smith. "Everybody loves Jell-O and Jell-O Puddings"

The JELL-O That Doesn't Jiggle

After years of railing against "dyspepsia-producing puddings" in its advertising, the Jell-O company started making its own brand of it in 1932.

It's not hard to figure out why.

Despite Jell-O's repeated warnings, people were still eating puddings. And if pudding lacks gelatin's glamour and jiggle, it's otherwise so similar to flavored gelatin desserts as to make it a logical business extension. Today, in fact, pudding products make up 45 percent of all Jell-O sales.

Whether it's to combat pudding's plain-Janeness or for some other reason, Jell-O pudding ad campaigns have often featured celebrities.

The Johnny-come-lately pudding was more of a tag line to Jell-O gelatin ads on Jack Benny's show. Kate Smith plugged both products almost equally in magazine ads and on her radio show (discussed in more detail in

Chapter 4), but the weight of visual evidence led most people to believe she favored the more indulgent product.

This was confirmed by a 1944 *Ladies' Home Journal* ad entitled "The Most Heartfelt Commercials on the Air" in which Smith "thrills a small admirer with an invitation to join her in her dressing room" for a "supper" of Jell-O pudding and Sanka Coffee (another General Foods product Smith hawked).

"I guess it's just that I enjoy good things to eat myself. So naturally I like to talk about 'em to other folks," Smith explains to the little girl before they dig into a huge bowl of "satisfying" Jell-O chocolate pudding.

In the 1994 film *Corrina, Corrina*, set in the '50s, romance blooms between a widowed adman and his housekeeper (played by Whoopi Goldberg) when she helps him come up with a new jingle for Jell-O Instant Pudding. A big advertising blitz also accompanied the actual early '50s introduction of that product. It included an award-winning cartoon by the *New Yorker*'s Saul Steinberg that featured grating music and an agitated housewife to illustrate its Busy Day Dessert theme.

Other instant pudding ads, reminiscent of the very first Jell-O Girl ones, showed children preparing their

Diced Raspberry

own pudding. One ended with kids placing a big bowl of pudding on the floor for the family cat.

For a full week in December 1953, General Foods forsook all its other products to air these and other ads on television. "Red Buttons and Our Miss Brooks quit drinking coffee, Roy Rogers and the Rocket Rangers performed their feats without the benefit of Post cereals, Mama chatted her way into a brand-new commercial and Bob Hope went down to the grocery store to see a new eye-catching shelf display," the General Foods company newsletter reported.

"Say kids, did I ever show you my gun?" Roy Rogers said as he pulled out his Colt in the now-startling introduction to his ad. "It's the first gun that could shoot six bullets without reloading," he boasted before moving on to another name you "can count on": Jell-O.

"They just make the best-tasting desserts in the whole world. . . . Next time you and your mom go shopping, make sure and look for that name," he said before launching into this song:

Oh it's never too late to make dessert,
With Jell-O Instant Pudding.
[One of Roy's kids]: So easy a kid can make dessert,
with Jell-O Instant Pudding.
[Roy and kids]: So get the busy day dessert,
Jell-O Instant Pudding.

The ads worked so well that less than a year later Jell-O introduced two new instant pudding flavors with a Maurice Sendak cartoon. It showed a little boy based on one in the picture book *A Very Special House* dancing, singing, and riding a Jell-O box "pony" before falling asleep to dream of the new lemon and banana cream flavors. Sendak's career-making *Where the Wild Things Are* was still to come but Jell-O's "Prancing Boy" won him early attention and acclaim.

Jell-O pudding was also advertised on classic '60s television shows such as *Green Acres*, *Gomer Pyle USMC*, and *The Andy Griffith Show*, often by their in-character cast members. In one Andy Griffith ad, Andy defends son Opie's idea of feeding pudding to his horse to a skeptical—and hungry—Deputy Barney Fife (Don Knotts).

"Don't you believe there's a horse who could enjoy Jell-O chocolate puddin' on account it's so nutritious

'cause they make it with milk?" Andy asks as a horse pokes his head through an open window behind Andy and Knott's eyes bug out.

"Try Jell-O puddin'. It's g—ooooo—d," the oblivious Andy finishes.

Even more memorable was the wacky series starring *Hollywood Squares* regular Paul Lynde that spoofed celebrity product endorsements. In one Lynde plays a "famous Olympic swimming champ" who wears scuba gear because "the water is way over my head." In another commercial gag, tennis star Lynde's opening line to his on-camera interviewer is: "OK, what do you want me to endorse?" The one where he played a Jell-O- pudding–loving equestrian ended with Lynde's leering suggestion, "If you give me another helping, I'll let you ride my pony."

Copywriter Al Hampel said Lynde was not an easy sell with Jell-O executives and it's not difficult to imagine why (especially in that pre-*Ellen* era). But Hampel says the ads scored record numbers for audience retention. In fact, he says he still runs into people who remember them.

Of course no discussion of Jell-O pudding advertising would be complete without at least mentioning Bill Cosby, who promoted Jell-O pudding and its extensions exclusively until 1990, when his role was broadened to include Jell-O gelatin. But mention is all we are going to do. (See Chapter 5 for a complete discussion of Cosby's work for Jell-O.) Right now we're going to talk instead about pudding premiums and extensions.

In 1972 Jell-O executives offered two interesting premiums, a Hasbro doll that came with cookware and a box of Jell-O Instant Pudding that was inexplicably named Sweet Cookie; and a pudding shaker designed by quintessential '60s pop artist Peter Max.

Remember Jell-O Soft Swirl, Whip 'n Chill, and Spoon Candy? We didn't think so. They were all variations on basic Jell-O pudding. (Soft Swirl was an upscale pudding; Whip 'n Chill, similar to a mousse; and Spoon Candy, pudding with a hard chocolate topping.) But you probably do remember such successful pudding spin-offs as No-Bake Cheesecake, Jell-O Pudding Cups, and Jell-O Pudding Pops.

The cheesecake was introduced with a 1967 Clio Award–winning ad in which a talkative Louise Lasser observes her taciturn husband eating a slice. In fact, the husband doesn't say a word during the entire ad and only smiles after the last bite.

"He likes it," she says with a sigh of relief. That line went on to even greater renown in the 1972 Mikey Life Cereal commercial; Lasser, to become Mary Hartman of the 1976 cult hit, *Mary Hartman, Mary Hartman*, and

Jell-O Cheesecake to become the flagship of Jell-O's still growing No Bake Dessert line.

Jell-O frozen Pudding Pops were also a huge hit when they were introduced in 1982—a situation, in part, created by an appealing ad featuring some pint-size legislators lobbying for their favorite Jell-O Pudding Pop varieties. "All in flavor, say yum," Speaker Cosby demands at the end.

Nevertheless, low-profit margins led Jell-O to discontinue this popular product in 1993.

Jell-O came out with pudding in single-serve cans in 1972 to compete with a similar product from Hunt's. Refrigerated pudding snacks only became a practical possibility for General Foods when it acquired Oscar Mayer and its system of supplying supermarkets with refrigerated foods in 1981. In 1985, General Foods built a whole new Mason City, Iowa, plant just to make them.

The most recent Jell-O pudding incarnation required neither refrigeration nor spoon. They were individually wrapped cakelike snack bars filled with pudding, called Jell-O Dessert Delights.

JELL-O Pudding Pops Reincarnated

You can't buy Jell-O Pudding Pops anymore but you can still make them. Here's how.

2 cups cold milk
1 package Jell-O Instant Pudding & Pie Filling, any flavor

Pour milk into medium bowl. Add pudding mix. Beat with wire whisk 1 minute. Pour pudding mixture into 6 5-ounce paper cups. Insert wooden popsicle stick (available at craft shops) into each cup for a handle. Freeze 5 hours or overnight, until firm. Free pops from cup by holding bottom of cup under warm running water for 15 seconds. Press on bottom of cup to push the pop out rather than twisting or pulling on the stick.

ALTERNATIVE FOR LAZY PERSONS: Purchase 6-pack of refrigerated Jell-O Pudding Snacks. Remove foil lid and insert wooden popsicle stick. Follow above directions for freezing and removing cups.

JELL-O Slogans

1932 Jell-O again
1935 New extra-rich flavor
1937 Look for the big red letters on the box
1941 America's favorite gelatin dessert

Chapter 4

MOLDING A SUCCESS

*T*he association of Jell-O gelatin with Jack Benny . . . is considered by trade observers to have been perhaps the greatest factor in recent years in building Jell-O sales to their present staggering total," the magazine *Modern Packaging* concluded some eight years after the two had parted.

But it wasn't the only factor.

Benny's wasn't even the only show to advertise Jell-O-brand gelatin during this period. Jell-O also sponsored *The Aldrich Family* when it debuted as Benny's summer replacement series, and after it joined Benny in the regular series' top ten. The show centered on sixteen-year-old Henry Aldrich, a boy who could turn a simple trip to the store into a town-wide disaster. Every week for thirteen years, Henry's long-suffering mother summoned mayhem into America's homes with this plaintive cry: "Hen-ree! Henry Aldrich!" To which cracked-voiced Henry would reply: "Com-ming Mother!"

Almost as famous was the Jell-O jingle sung by the entire cast:

Oh, the big red letters stand for the Jell-O family;
Oh, the big red letters stand for the Jell-O family;
That's Jell-O!
Yum-yum-yum!

Thoroughly Modern JELL-O

Jell-O sales during the '30s also got a boost from the electric refrigerator, which debuted in 1918 and was in enough homes by 1929 to merit its own Jell-O recipe booklet. One of the *Jell-O Secrets for the Automatic Refrigerator* therein revealed: putting Jell-O in the freezer compartment could cut its setting time in half.

Gelatin will actually set without refrigeration— early Jell-O ads suggested putting it in the sink, and many people used root cellars, wells, snow piles, and, later, their iceboxes—but Jell-O was one of those foods that benefited from a refrigerator's temperature consistency. For a time, serving Jell-O became a sign that you owned a refrigerator and therefore had money. Refrigerators made Jell-O seem modern and once again, like something of a status symbol.

A Change of Course

Jell-O sales also benefited from its growing popularity as a salad ingredient.

Although originally introduced as a dessert, the salad-making possibilities of Jell-O and the other convenience gelatins soon became evident. All of the major turn-of-the-century cookbooks offered recipes for tomato aspic, for instance. One of the first gelatin salad creations to gain wide popularity was Perfection Salad, a jellied coleslaw that won Mrs. John E. Cooke of New Castle, Pennsylvania, third prize of a sewing machine in a 1905 Knox Gelatine

JELL-O and Post-war America: An Author's View

Don DeLillo's epic treatise on postwar America, *Underworld*, includes a profile of a stereotypical suburban family that begins with a description of a mother making Jell-O.

Erica Deming "did things with Jell-O that took people's breath away." Even as she prepared her Jell-O chicken mousse and her husband polished the car, there were nine individual parfait glasses filled with multiple diagonal stripes of Jell-O in the refrigerator. Doing things with Jell-O almost always cheered Erica, DeLillo writes.

But there is trouble in gelatin paradise. It includes one missile-shaped Jell-O mold—a phallic reminder of the Cold War—that Erica owned but never used because it "made her feel uneasy somehow." Then there is her son Eric's dis-ease with Erica's tilted Jell-O desserts.

"It was as if a science-fiction force had entered the house and made some things askew while sparing others," Eric ponders.

Then there was the day Erica came home and found Eric with his head in her Jell-O antipasto salad. He told her he was trying to eat it from the inside out to test a scientific theory but she wondered if it wasn't something perverse. The story does show Eric to be almost as obsessed with masturbating as his mother is with Jell-O.

Incidentally, this piece was first published in the September 8, 1997, *New Yorker* as "Sputnik: A Small Tribute to Jell-O, the Most American of American Foods . . ."

Recipe for Postwar Suburban Bliss

Here's the recipe for the Jell-O chicken mousse
Erica Deming prepared for her family in
Underworld. The book did not win the National
Book Critics Circle Award for its cuisine, so
you're on your own with this.

3 cups chicken broth

2 small (3-ounce) packages or 1 large (6-ounce) package
    lemon Jell-O gelatin

1 teaspoon salt

$1/8$ teaspoon cayenne

3 tablespoons vinegar

1 $1/3$ cups whipped topping mix (like Cool Whip)

$2/3$ cup mayonnaise

2 cups cooked chicken, finely diced

2 cups celery, finely chopped

2 tablespoons pimiento, chopped

Bring 2 cups of the broth to a boil. Pour over
gelatin, salt, and cayenne, stirring until gelatin is
dissolved. Add remaining broth and the vinegar.
Chill until slightly thickened. Blend together
whipped topping and mayonnaise. Fold in
chicken, celery, and pimiento, and chill. Fold
thickened gelatin into chicken mixture, blending
well. Spoon into a 9 x 5-inch loaf pan. Chill until
firm. Unmold. Serve on crisp lettuce. Serves 6 as
an entrée; 9 to 12 as a side salad.

recipe contest judged by a panel that included Fannie
Farmer.

And, indeed, this salad was in many ways the
perfect embodiment of domestic scientists' beliefs
about what food should be. Molded salads were pretty,
light, sweet, and neat, and each year after 1910, recipes
for them made up an increasingly larger part of the
salad sections of Farmer's and other cookbooks.

Gelatin salads really came into their own in the
'30s. By then, almost a third of the salad recipes in any
cookbook were gelatin-based. General Foods watched
salad use move lemon Jell-O from fourth to second in
the flavor hierarchy and then, in 1930, introduced
lime specifically for salads. Soon afterward the
company heralded lime's arrival in *The Farmer's Wife*
magazine.

"Jell-O Salads, Welcome!, say the women of
America! Shimmering . . . luscious . . . Jell-O salads
are making this a salad nation!" its headline screamed.

It was true, and the reasons were easy to see. Jell-O
was a godsend to depression-era women struggling to
feed their families. At three boxes for twenty-five
cents, Jell-O was cheap. Jell-O salads in particular
were a spiffy way to dress up yesterday's table scraps, as
this 1930 *Farmer's Wife* ad pointed out.

"Open the cupboard door and peep in . . . What
do you see? A bit of fish? . . . a little meat . . . or cake
. . . some grape juice? . . . scarcely enough to serve
more than one or two persons? Then lend an ear to
Jell-O's magic! For Jell-O can make those tiny
portions into . . . delicious dishes to serve six to eight

persons! Out of next to nothing at all, Jell-O can help you contrive surprises that your family will prefer to many a far more expensive dish."

Despite the low cost, Jell-O was elegant enough to serve at the bridge or garden club meetings then filling women's social needs.

"Discovered! How to 'live high' on very little!" enticed one ad from this era. "The . . . recipes on this page possess tea room cleverness . . . Yet the cost . . . ridiculously small!" Among the featured recipes: Perfection Salad ("a delicious vitamin-rich salad for a few pennies a serving!") and Jell-O Cheese Loaf ("Cheese glorified—a 'company' treat at next to no cost!").

Energized by the possibilities of a new menu addition, Jell-O home economists produced recipes for the still-popular Under-the-Sea (lime Jell-O, pears, and cream cheese) and Golden Glow or Sunshine salads (lemon Jell-O, pineapple, and shredded carrots) as well as congealed Waldorf and jellied tuna, chicken, and corned beef salads.

Victory Dessert

Stretching and saving with Jell-O continued into the '40s but with the important new purpose of conserving food for America's wartime effort.

At the time Jell-O was sponsoring a radio variety show starring Kate Smith—not a woman who looked like she let a lot of food go to waste. In one ad she suggested disguising leftovers in a downscale version of a restaurant dessert cart she called the Jell-O Variety Tray. Its offerings included bruised fruit hidden in Jell-O gelatin and stale cinnamon toast topped with Jell-O pudding.

The company also put out a booklet of Jell-O recipes specifically designed to help housewives cope under rationing. *Bright Spots for Wartime Meals: 66 Ration-Wise Recipes* was narrated by a patriotic cartoon housewife named Victorianna who boasted of being able to turn a single apple into dessert for five. She offered recipes for victory garden vegetables, plentiful meats like tongue, and one-crust pies.

These pies were popular because shortening was rationed and they only needed half as much. Pudding and gelatin were natural fillings. Chiffon pies made by combining pudding or gelatin with whipped egg whites (and later, when the safety of raw egg whites was called into question, with whipped frozen evaporated milk, whipped cream, or Cool Whip) became so popular as to merit their own section in the 1943 *Joy of Cooking*.

Smart wartime housewives also bought Jell-O

because it did not require any rationing coupons. Sugar did but Jell-O—which is about 83 percent sugar—did not. Plagued with the same wartime sugar shortages as housewives, General Foods was forced to cut back sharply on Jell-O production.

To ease customers' frustration, General Foods hired *New Yorker* cartoonist Helen Hokinson to draw cartoons of her famous club women coping with the Jell-O shortage. The company ran these in the corner of Jell-O recipe ads until as late as 1946. In one typical of the series, a woman spots a Jell-O carton peeking out of a stranger's grocery bag and tells her friend, "Better hold my hands, Mary—or ask her to cover up that Jell-O!"

A Dessert for Every Decade

Here are three of the most popular Jell-O recipes from the '30s, '40s, and '50s.

'30s: Under-the-Sea Salad

1 can (16 ounces) pear halves in syrup, undrained

1 cup boiling water

1 (3-ounce) package lime Jell-O gelatin

$^1/_4$ teaspoon salt (optional)

1 tablespoon lemon juice

2 (3-ounce) packages cream cheese, softened

$^1/_8$ teaspoon ground cinnamon (optional)

Drain pears, reserving $^3/_4$ cup of the syrup. Dice pears; set aside. Stir boiling water into gelatin and salt in medium bowl at least 2 minutes until completely dissolved. Stir in reserved syrup and lemon juice. Pour 1 $^1/_4$ cups into 8 x 4 loaf pan or 4-cup mold. Refrigerate about 1 hour or until set but not firm (should stick to finger when touched and should mound).

Meanwhile, stir remaining gelatin gradually into cream cheese in large bowl with wire whisk until smooth. Stir in pears and cinnamon. Spoon over gelatin layer in pan. Refrigerate 4 hours or until firm. Unmold. Garnish with cinnamon, if desired. Serves 6.

'40s: Lemon Chiffon Pie

1 (3-ounce) package lemon Jell-O gelatin

1 $^1/_4$ cups boiling water

1 cup sugar

$^1/_2$ cup lemon juice

2 teaspoons finely grated lemon zest

1 (13-ounce) can evaporated milk, chilled

1 large baked pie shell or vanilla wafer or graham cracker crust

Dissolve Jell-O in boiling water. Add sugar. Let cool to room temperature before adding lemon juice and zest. Refrigerate until consistency of raw egg whites, about 30 minutes. Whip evaporated milk in large bowl at high speed until stiff. Reduce speed to medium, add gelatin mixture, then raise speed to high and beat until fluffy. Pour into pie shell or crust. Chill several hours or until set.

'50s: Parfait Pie

1 cup water

1 (3-ounce) package Jell-O gelatin, any flavor

1 pint vanilla ice cream, softened

1 $^1/_2$ cups sliced fruit (to complement the gelatin)

1 (9-inch) graham cracker pie crust

Bring water to a boil. Add gelatin; stir to dissolve. Stir in ice cream until melted. Chill 5 minutes. Add fruit. Pour into crust. Chill until firm.

48

Now's the time for **JELL-O**
SIX DELICIOUS FLAVORS

When a bunch of youngsters get together, there's
bound to be some gay goings-on! And there's bound
to be some big dishes of Jell-O ready and waiting
for them to dig into—if there's a wise "mom" in
the house! Jell-O gelatin desserts always cost so
little . . . and always please so much!

It's National Jell-O-to-Drink-Is-Even-Better-Than-You-Think Week!

Or if you never think—about Jell-O to drink, that is—it's
time you did. Why shouldn't the most refreshing, most delightful
dessert in the world make the most delightfully refreshing drink?
And what could be better for always-thirsty children than coolers
made of wholesome, thrifty Jell-O?

It's child's play to fix, too. Just dissolve a package of Jell-O in one
cup hot water. Pour in 3 cups cold water and lots of ice. Nothing
to add, nothing to do now, except sit back and let "little blotters"
drink up all they want.

WAIT . . . don't forget to save a cold one for yourself!

Don't let this week go by without JEL

Fifties Fun

The first major advertising campaign of the '50s featured the work of some of Hokinson's colleagues at the *New Yorker* and other well-known cartoonists. The idea echoed Jell-O's use of famous illustrators in the '20s, but reflected America's postwar optimism. Hank Ketcham showed a man breaking up a fight between Dennis the Menace and one of his school chums, the **Berenstains of Berenstains Bear fame drew an out-of-control kids' Halloween party**, and *New Yorker* cartoonist Syd Hoff showed a woman receiving a marriage proposal all under the umbrella theme, "Now's the time for Jell-O."

The lighthearted mood continued with "National Jell-O Weeks," a campaign spoofing a popular store promotional strategy of the time. They included National Jell-O-with-Fruit-to-Boot Week, National Trim-Your-Torso-With-Jell-O Week, and both National Be-the-First-on-Your-Block-to-Have-Jell-O-for-Breakfast Week and National Kids-Just-Love-to-Sprinkle-Jell-O-on-Cereal Week.

"You eat fruit in the morning, why not some tangy fruit flavored Jell-O?" the First-on-Your-Block one reasoned, at least semiseriously. The other suggested sprinkling Jell-O powder straight from the box on cereal, pudding, ice cream—even buttered toast.

TV Dessert

The Jell-O weeks TV ads, including an animated skit of a husband who was too henpecked to celebrate National Bellow-for-Jell-O Week, aired on *I Love Lucy*, *Hennesey* (starring Jackie Cooper), and *Lunch with Soupy Sales*. (Jell-O also sponsored Bob Hope's radio and television shows in the early '50s but none of these celebrity associations stuck the way it did for Jack Benny.)

The most famous Jell-O TV ad from this period was unrelated to the weeks campaign. This Clio Award—winning animated spot evoked the tone of a Chinese fable to tell the story of a poor Chinese baby whose chopsticks prevent him from enjoying the "famous Western delicacy, Jell-O" until he is given another "great Western invention," the spoon. "So end the ancient Chinese pantomime. Pretty good commercial, no?" the heavily accented narrator asks just before Chinese bells sound the crescendo Jell-O theme.

A companion print ad that ran about the same time featuring American Indian squaw and papoose puppets was just as charming—and to modern ears, just as un-PC. "Jell-O . . . top favorite in every American tepee! . . . Keeps papoose off the warpath. . . . Makes Big Chief Rain-in-the-Face smile in the face because it takes such little wampum."

"Superficially childlike but adult and modern" was how Young & Rubicam described their next major ad campaign of rewritten nursery rhymes. In the Jell-O versions of the classic rhymes, Little Miss Muffet said, "Away with these curds and whey; Jell-O's mighty nutritious and far more delicious"; and the moon that the cow jumped over "was all yellow, and *yum-m* made of Jell-O, so the cow went back for a spoon."

The animal ads that followed ran in *Life* and the *Saturday Evening Post* rather than children's magazines, and punned like so: The bee likes Jell-O

"beecause Jell-O's such a honey of a dessert"; for the leopard, Jell-O "really hits the spot."

The company offered framable copies of twelve of the animal ads (minus the advertising copy) and a Jell-O animal coloring book as consumer premiums. General Foods also created figurines based on both campaigns that they gave away to their top three thousand dealers. Today these hand-painted Sebastian Miniatures sell for $350 to $450 each, placing them among the most valuable Jell-O collectibles. As for the cow creamer that Sebastian designed for National Jell-O-with-Cream Week offered to consumers for $1 and a Jell-O label: They now go for $250 or $300 each.

These ads featured no recipes. Only one Jell-O recipe book was published in the '50s—*It's Dessert Time* in 1953. There was really no need, when regular cookbooks and women's magazines were filled with gelatin recipes.

Techno-Powder

Jell-O was the beneficiary of the processed food school of cooking that sprung up after the war. Companies that had developed frozen vegetables and orange juice for foxhole consumption advertised like crazy to get housewives to cook with these new convenience foods. As one of America's first convenience foods, Jell-O needed no such introduction. At the same time Jell-O looked like some of the popular new plastics hitting the market and blended well with other convenience ingredients (General Foods' own Minute Rice and Dream Whip among them).

Unmasking Your
MOLDING FEARS

What was behind the '60s trend of decorating the kitchen with gelatin molds? In some cases, it might have been because people thought they were pretty. But we think many of these mold decorations were the result of the widely recognized psychiatric malady, unmoldaphobia—the fear of not being able to get a gelatin dessert out of its mold.

Anyone who has ever made more than one or two gelatin molds can tell you about a time when the gelatin wouldn't release. Karen Johnson of Columbus, Ohio, has a more horrific story than usual. She was attending a party where the host was having problems unmolding her spectacular Jell-O creation. Because Johnson is a home economist, she was summoned into the kitchen to help.

"I tried to rescue the pièce de résistance by repeating everything the host had tried," Johnson told freelance writer Grace Howaniec in 1997. That included immersing the mold in warm water, wrapping it in a hot towel, and inserting the knife tip to the side to release air.

"I was holding the mold over the sink, inserting the tip of the knife, when the mold came out with a sudden whoosh and slid right down her [garbage] disposal."

Here are some kitchen-tested tips to save you from this fate.

 Decrease the cold water you use in the recipe by one-fourth.

That means if you're making a normal eight-serving gelatin dish, use one and a half cups of cold water instead of two cups. (Some gelatin recipes designed for molds already make this adjustment.) Do not use the speed-set method (adding ice cubes) to make the gelatin since it never sets as firmly.

 Spray the inside of the mold with vegetable oil cooking spray or grease it with a light layer of butter or mayonnaise before pouring in the Jell-O. The surface of your mold won't be as shiny but which would you rather do—serve an intact mold with a slightly dull finish or one with unsightly broken pieces?

 Make sure the Jell-O fills the mold. Half-filled gelatin molds are almost impossible to get out in one piece. Most gelatin recipes will tell you the cup-size mold required. Premeasure your mold by pouring in cups of water. Incidentally, almost any clean pan or container can be used as a mold—including empty coffee and pineapple cans (which you can poke holes into to break the vacuum come unmolding time).

The moment of truth: First make sure the gelatin is completely firm (it should not be sticky on top). Then dip the mold up to its rim for fifteen seconds in warm water (not hot or it might melt!). Work your fingers between the gelatin and the sides of the mold a bit. Moisten a chilled serving plate with water. (This will make it easier to center the mold.) Put plate on top of mold and then turn it upside down and shake. At this point—if you're lucky and have followed all these suggestions—you should hear a blessed whoosh and a kerplop.

In fact, convenience food cookery may very well have found its highest expression in Jell-O. A casserole made by emptying cans of green beans, cream of mushroom soup, and french fried onion rings into a dish might taste good but it wasn't beautiful, like Jell-O. Those same ingredients could not also be used to make entrées, salads, or desserts, like Jell-O could.

Jell-O's versatility and moldability had always inspired creativity but never more so than in the '50s. It may be that all the time women were (supposedly) saving by using instant rice and frozen spinach was being used for gelatin masterpieces. Sometimes they even put the instant rice and frozen spinach in the gelatin. But more common were vegetables floating in lime-green wreaths. Cream cheese and chopped nuts suspended in ripe red mounds. Horseradish and vinegar lurking in a beet-lemon Jell-O suspension. Strawberry crowns studded with maraschino cherry rubies. Crushed pineapple and miniature marshmallows floating in light green clouds. Layers of Jell-O color alternating with layers of cream.

In the '50s, there wasn't much else a hostess could produce that was quite as impressive.

One Jell-O dessert wowing people at the time was Parfait Pie, a one-crust wonder made by mixing unset flavored gelatin with softened ice cream or sherbet that debuted in *Better Homes and Gardens* in 1952 and is still popular.

Three years later one R. J. Gatti wrote General Foods with the idea for another Jell-O classic. Crown Jewel Dessert features different colored cubes of Jell-O set off against a backdrop of Cool Whip so that it resembles stained glass. (In fact, the dish is also known as Jell-O Stained Glass or

Crown Jewel JELL-O

This dessert is still a stunner even forty-one years after it was first introduced.

3 (3-ounce) packages Jell-O gelatin in contrasting, complementary flavors and colors
1 (3-ounce) package lemon Jell-O gelatin
1 cup hot pineapple juice
1 3/4 cups Cool Whip or whipped cream

Prepare 3 Jell-O flavors of your choice separately, using 1 cup boiling water and 1/2 cup cold water for each. Pour into separate greased 8 x 8 pans and chill until set, about 4 hours. Cut each into 1/2-inch cubes.

Dissolve the lemon Jell-O in the pineapple juice, and then add 1/2 cup cold water. Keep in the mixing bowl until it starts to set (about 45 minutes). Blend the Cool Whip or whipped cream with the partially set lemon Jell-O. Fold in the gelatin cubes and pour into a greased 9-inch tube pan. Chill until firm (at least 4 hours). Unmold and cut into slices. Serves 10 to 12.

Broken Glass.) It was beautiful and offered the added benefit of requiring the purchase of multiple packages of Jell-O. General Foods paid Gatti ten dollars, made

a few revisions, and unveiled the new dessert two years later at Jell-O's sixtieth birthday party in LeRoy, with Mrs. New York State serving the slices.

The Joys of JELL-O Cookery

Crown Jewel was only one of the most spectacular of four thousand Jell-O dessert recipes the home economists had squirreled away during an eight-year cookbook publishing hiatus. In 1961, General Foods decided to bring the best of these together into the *The Joys of Jell-O* cookbook. At 95 pages and 250 recipes it was by far the largest Jell-O recipe collection the company had ever attempted.

Its photographs showed fruit floating like astronauts and salad molds that looked like stylish skyscrapers.

By 1966, more than 2 million Jell-O-hungry consumers had sent in a quarter and fruit pictures from six Jell-O cartons (or fifty cents and three pictures, or twelve pictures and no money) to get one of the first eight editions of *Joys* (eventually there would be eleven) and thus gain access to wonders such as barbecue Jell-O salad, Jell-O popcorn balls, Jell-O marzipan candy, Jell-O glaze for roast duck, and "ring-around-the" recipes for both fruit and tuna. There was also a Jell-O banana-peanut salad, introduced as something to serve "with, after, and between meals" (which pretty much covered all possibilities). The "Tips and Tricks" section explained how to place stemmed glasses between bars of the refrigerator rack so the gelatin would set at a slant for that extra "touch of creativity." The provocatively titled "Two-Way" chapter was actually about recipes that could be served as either salads or desserts. How to cue guests to the difference? "When you serve them as desserts, garnish with prepared whipped topping or whipped cream. As salads, unmold them on crisp greens and top with mayonnaise or salad dressing," its introduction explained.

The "There's Always Room" Campaign

The most successful Jell-O ad campaign of the '60s focused on Jell-O's lightness. With the economy booming and tables groaning, the success of this

Joys Reincarnated for the Cyber Age

The Joys of Jell-O cookbook is the inspiration for one of the most helpful Jell-O cooking sites on the World Wide Web.

Bachelor computer programmer Andy Oakland first encountered a 1963 edition of the cookbook classic at a friend's house in 1995 and was so amused by its "insanely overwrought" prose and "glowing and garish" photos that he decided to post a few of its weirder recipes on the Web alongside a retro clip-art cartoon of himself as Chef Andy.

The e-mails started rolling in almost immediately asking for recipes. A recipe for strawberry jam made with Jell-O and figs. A recipe for a dish someone's grandmother used to make with cottage cheese and dry Jell-O powder. A recipe for a red- Jell-O-and-ice-cream ring remembered from a childhood birthday party.

After dutifully retrieving and posting recipes for the women (visitors are almost all female), Chef Andy the Jell-O jokester quickly became Chef Andy the Jell-O Ann Landers, along the way producing one of the best collections of retro Jell-O recipes on paper or screen. Would you believe Citrus Surprise ("even good for breakfast!"), Pink Party Dessert (made with stale angel food cake), and Rhubarb Dump Cake (recipe below)?

Disappointed about his lack of dates—he actually claims the real reason was lack of time to do things besides Jell-O recipe research—Oakland added a bulletin board to Chef Andy's Jell-O Pages (www.chefandy.com) in 1999 with the intention of letting Jell-O recipe seekers help one another.

But when Oakland recently signed on to his server after a two-month absence there were no fewer than four hundred messages for Chef Andy—the impersonal cyber fence apparently considered no substitute for a smiling cartoon Jell-O expert.

Rhubarb Dump Cake

Recipes for cakes made by adding gelatin powder to a cake mix or pouring dissolved Jell-O over a baked cake poked full of holes (poke cake) are fairly common. But Chef Andy's Web site is the only place I've ever seen a recipe for a Jell-O dump cake.

5 cups rhubarb, diced
1 cup sugar
1 (3-ounce) package raspberry Jell-O gelatin
3 cups miniature marshmallows
1 (18.5-ounce) package white cake mix
2 eggs
Whipped cream

Arrange rhubarb in bottom of 9 x 13 pan. Sprinkle with sugar and gelatin. Cover with marshmallows. Prepare cake mix using 2 eggs and required amount of water. Spread batter over the mixture. Bake at 350° for 50 to 55 minutes. Serve warm with whipped cream. Serves 8.

approach made sense. This was also a time when dessert was the expected ending to every meal, even ones so huge and heavy that it was hard to think about eating another bite.

"These are people who like to eat," a narrator began over footage of families sitting down to enjoy a big feed. One ad in the series showed a Maine family eating seafood; another, an Italian clan; still another, a family celebrating their son's first visit home since enlisting in the military. The mood was extremely realistic, from dialogue that seemed unscripted to actors that actually looked unattractive.

"Have they been feeding you good, son?" a man asks his enlisted son.

"Great dad, the food is fabulous, really fabulous," says the new recruit.

"You don't look it," his mother says skeptically before attempting to make up for the lost calories in one meal.

"You're feeding me too much," the boy protests when she goes back to the kitchen to get dessert. But he's relieved and delighted when he sees what it is.

"Oh, Jell-O!" he says before the narrator breaks in with the line that ended them all: "People who like to eat like Jell-O gelatin. There's always room for Jell-O."

The ads won awards for Young & Rubicam. "There's always room for Jell-O" became one of the most famous advertising slogans of all time. More than thirty years after it was dropped from Jell-O advertising it still crops up in jokes about the product

(including in *Ghostbusters 2* in 1989). Young & Rubicam even resurrected it in 1991.

The series also sent Jell-O sales soaring to new heights. But even as General Foods moved Jell-O's eastern operations from its LeRoy, New York, birthplace to a new dessert plant in Dover, Delaware, with plenty of room for growth, more convenient sweets were crowding the space that Jell-O always occupied on grocers' shelves. The "always" in the famous slogan didn't turn out to be a very long time after all.

JELL-O Innovations

1930. The congealed salad trend prompts the introduction of lime Jell-O. Nationally lime sales still soar on holidays, when the vast majority of non-Mormon salad molds are made.

1936. Jell-O takes on Knox with new Unflavored Jell-O Plain Gelatin. "Plain gelatin—modernized at last!" its ads exclaimed.

1942. Cola Jell-O becomes the seventh delicious flavor and, in its introductory ad, "the most glorious dessert surprise . . . in years!" It goes flat within the year.

BIG GROCERY NEWS! COLA FLAVOR JELL-O

The Rosenbergs: Condemned for Cutting Up a JELL-O Box

You've probably heard the story of Ethel and Julius Rosenberg, the couple who were executed in 1951 amid much controversy after being found guilty of furnishing information about the atomic bomb to the Soviets in the mid-'40s.

But did you know the key role Jell-O played in their conviction?

According to the FBI, based on testimony from three other people allegedly involved in the crime, Julius Rosenberg cut part of a Jell-O box into two odd-shaped pieces and gave one piece to his brother-in-law, David Greenglass, to use in identifying his Soviet spy courier. That courier, Harry Gold, would bear the matching piece and say the code phrase, "I come from Julius."

In fact, the government's case against the Rosenbergs rested almost entirely on the idea that Julius Rosenberg gave part of that Jell-O box to the Soviet agent who passed it to Gold.

This despite the fact that neither Gold nor Greenglass said anything about a Jell-O box when they were first arrested. Greenglass initially talked about a cut card and only later identified it as a Jell-O box. Gold only mentioned Jell-O after meeting up with Greenglass in jail.

Moreover, when Gold was originally questioned about the code phrase, he recalled it as being "something on the order of Bob sent me or Benny sent me or John sent me or something like that." (Benny—like the man whose show was sponsored by Jell-O for much of Gold's lifetime.) Gold only remembered the code phrase as "I come from Julius" after Rosenberg had been implicated by Greenglass. Gold also came to the Rosenberg trial with a spectacular history of lying.

Nevertheless, the government prosecution clung to the Jell-O box story, even producing a facsimile of it (an original was never found) to hold up at the trial.

Whether a real physical sign or just a story, the Jell-O box was loaded with meaning for Americans by this time, Harvard University professor Marjorie Garber argues in her 1995 essay "Jell-O," citing Norman Rockwell and patriotic wartime Jell-O ads.

For a group of Jews to use this ultimate symbol of patriotism, America, and white Anglo-Saxon Protestantism "as the supposed clue to a Communist conspiracy to deliver America and its free enterprise system into the hands of the Soviet Union ranks as the ultimate, if trivial, outrage," Garber writes.

Selling atomic secrets to the Soviets is bad enough but once Jell-O got dragged into it, the Rosenbergs didn't stand a chance.

1955. General Foods fuels '50s housewives' enthusiasm for molded salads with a new apple flavor that gets five of the six minutes of advertising time on the first televised broadcast of

Ringling Brothers' circus. A groan-inducing print ad features a gnu, who says, "When I'm eating Jell-O, I wish I were a gnu. Then when folks ask, 'What's new, gnu?' I'd answer, apple Jell-O."

1956. Johnny Carson, Lucille Ball, and Roy Rogers help introduce Jell-O's three new "deep, dark, delicious flavors": imitation black cherry, imitation grape, and imitation black raspberry. Jell-O shifted from natural to artificial flavorings for all but their citrus flavors in the '30s but in the technology-obsessed '50s, "imitation" becomes a proud part of the flavor name.

1958. The postwar baby boom prompts the debut of a new double-sized "family pack" of Jell-O in the three popular red flavors. By 1960, there are six-ounce boxes of eight flavors.

1961 to 1964. Blackberry, orange-pineapple, mixed fruit, lemon-lime, strawberry-banana, and pineapple-grapefruit flavors are introduced in rapid succession.

1964. After years of only changing flavors, Jell-O gelatin marketers break out of the proverbial mold with two big ideas: Jell-O Fruit Mold Supreme and Jell-O Salad Gelatin. Fruit Mold Supreme is a shelf-stable gel-and-fruit dessert that comes in its own aluminum mold. "To serve, just chill, open with a can opener and unmold—kerplop!—[for] a delectable dessert [or] delicious fruit salad," the ads explain. Fruit Mold Supreme's price tag of nine cents a serving or three times that of regular Jell-O could explain its short shelf life.

Directions for Jell-O Salad Gelatins call for fresh vegetables and vinegar as well as the more usual water. They come in celery, mixed vegetable, seasoned tomato, and Italian salad flavors, and only last about three years.

Unflavored Jell-O is reintroduced after a twenty-two-year hiatus as the only unflavored gelatin so refined that it doesn't taste like gelatin. The ad says, "New Jell-O Unflavored Gelatin has a lack of flavor all its own," and suggests drinking it to dampen appetites and strengthen fingernails. One ad even features a space to examine your hand and the question, "Should you be using Jell-O Unflavored Gelatin?" America answered no and by early 1966, Unflavored Jell-O was no more.

1965. Jell-O packaging expands along with the economy, producing new twelve-ounce variety packages of four red or citrus flavors in a single box, and new nine-ounce boxes of the big reds (now dubbed family sized but called snack size in 1971, when snack foods became the competition).

Mr. Wiggle, an artificially sweetened gelatin for children, is introduced after General Foods hears Pillsbury is about to go to market with a similar product named Jiggly. Ads in the Sunday comics tell kids that "Mr. Wiggle tastes like candy—but no sugar! So you can eat all you want, anytime you want."

General Foods produces animated TV ads and promotional giveaways (including puppets and an inflatable bag) featuring the bloblike Mr. Wiggle and Sweet-Toothed Sam, a villain always out to get Mr. Wiggle's dessert.

Pillsbury never does come out with Jiggly, and General Foods loses $3.3 million before discontinuing Mr. Wiggle and still ends up being sued by a consumer who wants "credit" for the idea.

1968. After flopping with the kids, General Foods introduces three new tart red flavors for adults— wild strawberry, wild raspberry, and wild cherry.

JELL-O Slogans

1941 Try the new Jell-O with the locked-in flavor
1945 Make it more and merrier with Jell-O
1946 Jell-O again
1951 America's red letter desserts
1952 Now's the time for Jell-O
1955 A Jell-O salad makes the meal
1956 Just for the fun of it—Jell-O tonight
1958 It's national . . . Jell-O week
1962 New Jell-O with the fresh fruit taste
1964 There's always room for Jell-O
1967 The refreshing dessert
1967 The best of everything
1967 Imagine tasting Jell-O for the first time
1968 Now Jell-O has the just-picked taste of fresh fruit
1968 How sweet it isn't

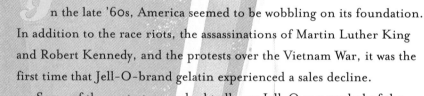

Chapter 5
WATCH IT WOBBLE, SEE IT JIGGLE

In the late '60s, America seemed to be wobbling on its foundation. In addition to the race riots, the assassinations of Martin Luther King and Robert Kennedy, and the protests over the Vietnam War, it was the first time that Jell-O-brand gelatin experienced a sales decline.

Some of the protesters undoubtedly saw Jell-O as a symbol of the establishment and corporate America. Of greater import for Jell-O sales was the huge increase in the number of women working outside the home and the corresponding decline in the time they had to make elaborate gelatin molds. Other changes impacting sales were the competition from new frozen-food novelties and already-made snack cakes, and the challenges posed by the gourmet and natural foods movements, whose bias against processed and convenience foods like Jell-O was now just starting to reach mainstream Americans.

High Concept Campaign

The then shaky future of Jell-O was reflected in the uncertain slogan attached to its first ad campaign of the '70s, "Somehow it's always right." The campaign starred the Fifth Dimension, the singing group flying high from their top ten hit about going "Up, Up and Away" in a balloon. So the Jell-O

people put the group on top of a giant Jell-O box and had them sing about "An easy touch of taste, that never gets too heavy . . ." When they got to the chorus ("Light as a cloud, Jell-O brand gelatin / Somehow it's always right . . ."), a Jell-O account executive crouching behind the box released a bunch of balloons.

The idea, recalls former Jell-O ad manager Dick Helstein, was to continue the light dessert theme that the "There's always room for Jell-O" campaign had started. But the execution was nowhere near as polished and viewers were left scratching their heads. "It got some of the highest numbers for recall and lowest for understanding of any Jell-O ad in history," Helstein says. It was also probably the only ad for any product to feature the word *gossamer.*

Taking on the Trends

Fortunately it was only one of many attempts Jell-O executives made to stem the sales slide. A method of preparing Jell-O with ice cubes had been introduced a number of years earlier. Although not a perfect

solution to Jell-O's time problem, it allowed a slightly soupy gelatin to be served in an hour. In 1964, the company introduced Fruit Mold Supreme, the short-lived, shelf-stable gel and fruit mold discussed in Chapter 4. They also ran ads that suggested women simply forgo the whole laborous gelatin-making process by sprinkling Jell-O on cupcakes, ice cream, and fruit. Other ads, bearing the tag line "Make someone happy. Make someone Jell-O" and featuring pictures of happy families eating it, seemed to urge women to return to their old people-pleasing role.

Jell-O's first attempt to combat competition from the new, more convenient desserts featured footage of a baseball stadium vendor hawking Jell-O in paper cups and the tag line "If it was there, you'd eat it." This only seemed to call attention to the problem. Subsequent ads simply called Jell-O a snack. The company also came out with a new twelve-ounce snack-size box (so-called because it contained enough Jell-O for dessert that night plus extra servings to snack on the next day) and suggested moms pour the Jell-O in portable paper cups. (In 1971, they even offered a premium of a multitiered snack tree that would keep the cups from taking up too much refrigerator space.)

As for the gourmet and natural foods crowd, they got a 1973 revision of *The Joys of Jell-O. The New Joys of Jell-O* pictured earth mothers and

The New Joys of Jell-O Gelatin Dessert *recipe book*

Poke cake

big-city sophisticates enjoying salad niçoise, salmon dill mousse, and wine gelatin, among other exotic dishes. (Noticeable by its absence was poke cake, a 1969 Kraft Kitchens invention made by poking holes in a baked cake and then pouring hot Jell-O over it to create beautiful interior Jell-O icicles. Beautiful but apparently not sophisticated enough for this edition.) In the parallel television ad, an Alice Waters–like Californian named Janet Bell sent her longhaired kids up a backyard tree for fresh oranges to make Jell-O fruit parfaits.

The Emotional Angle

By 1975, high inflation prompted a switch back to the value theme popular during World War II. The slogan "To make exciting meals on a budget, start with Jell-O gelatin" implied that Jell-O needed help to taste good. This failed to excite consumers or stem an eleven-year sales slide. (In 1968, American families bought 16 packages of Jell-O a year; by 1979, that figure had fallen to 11.4.) That same year, 1975, Young & Rubicam began interviewing consumers about their personal, positive experiences with the brand.

"There's a lot of affection for Jell-O," Young & Rubicam president Alexander Kroll told *Forbes* at the

time. "It's the name. It's Jack Benny. It's your mother serving it."

A group of Kroll's employees gathered at New York's UN Plaza Hotel with the results of this research and talked and ate Jell-O—and nothing but Jell-O—for several days. Their conclusion?

"Jell-O was not like the usual dessert. It was playful. It was engaging. It was fun," said John Ferrell, the Young & Rubicam employee in charge of the Jell-O retreat. And fun was best conveyed through music, Ferrell and his team believed.

Unfortunately, Ferrell reached this conclusion on his favorite lyricist's last day at the agency. John Nieman was literally packing up his things when Ferrell came into his office and begged him to write what turned out to be the most memorable jingle in Jell-O's advertising history: "Watch that wobble, / See that wiggle, / Taste that jiggle . . ."

The story that Ferrell and company built around Nieman's song was about a family reunion and began with the hostess's attention-getting admission: "I didn't make dessert." Shoulders sag before she adds, "I made some fun." The tune kicks in and three generations are shown interacting with their Jell-O and each other in quick, cola-commercial-like cuts.

Thanks in large part to the catchy music of Ed LeBunski (of "Nobody can do it like McDonald's can" fame) but also to Nieman's lyrics and the appealing actors, the "Cousins" ad won both industry and consumer awards and sent Jell-O sales rising again. Print ads and a spin wheel recipe premium included dishes consumers could serve at their own family gatherings. Regular boxed Jell-O sales increased 1.5 percent—but only for a short time.

Krafting a New Course

The long-term volume decline of about 2 percent a year continued through the late '80s. By 1987, the company was selling about half as many boxes as at the 1968 peak. During the '80s, the brand also suffered from image problems caused by the twin bar fads of alcoholic Jell-O shots and Jell-O wrestling, and management shake-ups in the wake of Philip Morris's 1985 purchase of General Foods and late-'80s merger with sister Philip Morris food company Kraft. But with cost reductions that kept Jell-O profits rising and new successes like Jell-O freezer pops and Sugar Free Jell-O with NutraSweet, nobody seemed to mind.

That attitude was reflected in the advice Dana Gioia received when he was named marketing manager for the brand in 1988. One predecessor offered: "Running this business is like piloting a big ship. You might be able to make slight adjustments in its movement here and there but don't expect any big changes or growth. Just keep it on course."

But Gioia was not interested in playing Captain Stubing. Instead he took another look at a study the company had commissioned in 1986 that showed a divide the size of a twenty-five-cup gelatin mold between the way younger and older women viewed gelatin desserts.

Jell-O's biggest fans were older women who still viewed dessert as an essential part of the meal. Younger women thought of sweets in terms of snacking and Jell-O as something for family gatherings. Not surprisingly, the recipes in 1987's ***Jell-O Pages*** ads and recipe booklets were introduced in terms of exactly these latter kinds of usages.

"I'm starving! How long until dinner?" was the booklet's lead-in to recipes for "light snacks" like Melon Bubble.

"Mom and Dad arrived two hours late. Their car had broken down and they were exhausted. They said they didn't want dinner but

when I brought out my Jell-O Gelatin Cheer 'Em Up Salad, you should have seen their appetites pick up . . ." read one of the ads.

Those consumers not addressed were the many young mothers whose work schedules left them little time to read magazines and recipe booklets. So Gioia and his colleagues began trying to reach them with a series of in-store ads and promotions.

JELL-O Poetics

What do Kool-Aid Man and Jell-O Jigglers have in common with the new formalist poetry? Dana Gioia, a former Jell-O marketing manager, who like T. S. Eliot and Wallace Stevens before him, led a double life as a serious poet.

For Gioia's first seven years at General Foods, it was also a secret life. "I worried if they found out I was a poet, they'd start checking my addition," he says. Then *Esquire* outed Gioia by naming him to a list of "Men and Women Under 40 Who Are Changing the Nation" for his leadership in the revival of formalist poetry (i.e., the kind that rhymes).

Shortly afterward, Gioia's "supermacho" boss called him into his office and asked if it was true. Gioia said it was.

"Shit," he said between cigar-clenched teeth in what Gioia took to be "the official corporate reaction."

Gioia was interested in poetry from very early on but, he jokes, "My parents never gave me the independent income I so richly deserved." As the son of a cabdriver and a telephone operator, "I aspired, God help me, to a middle-class life." So he went to Stanford Business School and after that to work on Kool-Aid at General Foods. After a couple of years in mergers and acquisitions, he became marketing manager for Jell-O, where his role in the wildly successful Jigglers campaign earned him a vice presidency.

Meanwhile, on weekends and evenings he was writing poetry. Although at least one critic attacked Gioia's work as a "poetry of money," it was far more often praised. "He writes with a kind of bright exactness that is lacking in a lot of poetry today," says Pulitzer Prize–winning poet Donald Justice.

Gioia also became famous for a 1991 essay in the *Atlantic Monthly* in which he questioned the insularity of the poetic community (a view no doubt influenced by his life apart). The essay, "Can Poetry Matter?," generated more responses than any other article in the *Atlantic*'s recent history and also became the basis of his National Book Critics Circle Award–nominated book of the same name.

Gioia says working at General Foods "grounded my poetry very much in the daily world" even as it shielded him from the need to write simply to make money. Now that he's left food marketing, he says he is applying the business skills he honed on Jell-O to his writing business—although he has as yet no plans to boost his poetry's kid appeal by spelling it out in Jell-O Jiggler letters.

Gioia knew that recipes motivate half of all Jell-O usage, so every day after lunch, the Jell-O marketing team gathered to eat Jell-O desserts from the General Foods kitchens. "A lot of them were incredibly delicious—but also incredibly complicated," Gioia remembers. "We were getting desperate when one day the cooks came in with something they called Jell-O squares. The first thing we noticed is that you could pick them up with your hands. And they tasted like gummy bears."

The squares also set in just an hour and required four times the usual amount of Jell-O. Gioia was further intrigued to hear they could be cut out into shapes with cookie cutters. Once Gioia determined that the recipe was easy enough even for him and the other MBAs to make, all that was left was to find a better name. The first time the word Jigglers came up during the brainstorming session, "We all laughed because it sounded kind of obscene. But we liked the alliteration. So we went around and asked the secretaries if they thought it was dirty." They said no, and Jigglers it became.

Sales Bounce Back

In spring of 1990, the Jigglers recipe launched a blitz of integrated marketing rarely seen in a company as large and with as many competing fiefdoms as Kraft General Foods. There were displays in supermarkets, the recipe on the box, Jiggler mold giveaways, Sunday newspaper drops, and ads targeted to kids, adults, and Hispanics—not to mention the first ad Bill Cosby did for Jell-O gelatin after his successful pudding commercials. It showed Cosby and some kids at a black-tie dinner throwing away their spoons over the Jell-O treat "we can eat with our bare hands."

One year later sixty-five thousand alphabet mold kits (discussed in a company newsletter as being sure to appeal to "today's achievement-minded parents") were mailed to teachers.

The initial Jigglers promotional blitz increased Jell-O sales by an astounding 47 percent and tripled recipe requests to the Jell-O 800 number.

Money

Money is a kind of poetry.—WALLACE STEVENS

Money, the long green,
cash, stash, rhino, jack
or just plain dough.

Chock it up, fork it over,
shell it out. Watch it
burn holes through pockets.

To be made of it! To have it
to burn! Greenbacks, double eagles,
megabucks and Ginnie Maes.

It greases the palm, feathers a nest,
holds heads above water,
makes both ends meet.

Money breeds money.
Gathering interest, compounding daily.
Always in circulation.

Money. You don't know where it's been,
but you put it where your mouth is.
And it talks.

—Dana Gioia

Even competitor Knox—whose own "finger" gelatin recipe dated back to 1917—reported a Jigglers sales bump, in part no doubt because at one point, the Jell-O factories could not keep up with the demand.

Although increases for the year were a more modest 7 percent, Jigglers did something even more important than bump sales: at a time when dessert was languishing, Jigglers transformed Jell-O into a kids' snack. It also turned Jell-O making into an opportunity for guilt-wracked working parents to do something fun with their kids.

In 1992, this idea of Jell-O as family activity became the focus of the new Snacktivities campaign in which cartoon kid Sammy and his dog Watson gave official sanction to "underground" favorites like Jell-O aquariums (made from berry blue Jell-O and gummy fish) and **dirt cups** (out of Jell-O pudding, gummy worms, and crushed Oreo "dirt").

DIRT CUPS
Dig in and spoon up a delicious snack.

Spring Growth

The introduction of molds for Jell-O Jiggler Easter eggs caused another big Jell-O sales spurt in 1995. Jiggler eggs got their federal blessing at the White House easter egg roll that year. Thanks to the Jiggler molds, Easter now rivals Thanksgiving as Jell-O's biggest holiday. But boomer nostalgia and the retro chic craze also boosted late-'90s Thanksgiving sales.

They also prompted a new *Joy of Jell-O Molds* cookbook and a new plastic mold giveaway of an old-fashioned, ornate design.

In the '90s, Jell-O marketing was split between adults and kids. An ad in which Bill Cosby, the Easter Bunny, and some kids sang of the dawn of a new "wiggly, jiggly Easter" ran almost simultaneously with the first of the "Still the Coolest" series of sophisticated first-person tributes to Jell-O flavors. One of the most amusing of these adult ads compared pictures of a kiwi and a bald head as a woman testifies to her love for both strawberry-kiwi Jell-O and her bald boyfriend.

White House Easter Egg Roll

As the '90s ended, the company told consumers to "juice up" their Jell-O by replacing fruit juice for the called-for cold water. The campaign was similar to a 1992 idea to make Refreshers with Jell-O and carbonated beverages that in the late '90s morphed into a new sub-line of Jell-O flavors designed specifically for that purpose.

Still Shaking After 100 Years

The first "sparkling" flavor—the champagnelike white grape—was introduced to celebrate Jell-O's 100th birthday in 1997 and unveiled at a party held at Cooper Union in New York City, the college founded by the man who obtained the first American patent for a gelatin dessert. Not long afterward, the brand broke with tradition by dropping its advertising agency of nearly three-quarters of a century in favor of Foote, Cone & Belding and a new campaign that included the phrase "Jell-O always breaks the mold."

Celebrating 100 YEARS OF JELL-O
America's Most Famous Dessert

JELL-O Jargon

Jog (pronounced like the running term): What Kraft marketing and sales people call boxes of Jell-O-brand gelatin.

Jogs: What these same people call refrigerated Jell-O gelatin snacks.

Jop: Insider acronym for Jell-O pudding.

Scroll: Word they use to refer to the best-selling Jell-O flavors: strawberry, cherry, raspberry, orange, lemon, and lime.

The Comic Who Launched a Billion JELL-O Purchases

It's not possible to separate the popularity and success of Jell-O from the popularity and success of Bill Cosby. Cosby has only been the third spokesman for the brand in more than one hundred years, and his twenty-seven years with Jell-O is reportedly the longest continuously running advertising deal between any celebrity and any product.

Jell-O has become a big part of Cosby's identity—so much so that it is the number-one source of jokes about him. Jell-O has not only been a major source of

income for Cosby but also one of creative satisfaction and visibility. So how did it all start?

Jell-O executives were facing a threat from Hunt's Snack Pack canned pudding when they first approached Cosby in 1973. Cosby's comedy routines about his childhood interested them more than his better-known role on *I Spy*. Former Jell-O advertising chief Dick Helstein remembers the early test ads as "trying to put Jell-O into Cosby's comedy [act]." But executives soon decided he worked better with real live kids. Indeed, some of

the best moments in Cosby's Jell-O ads have come not from Cosby or the ad copy but the interaction between him and the kids.

One of the most memorable moments happened in 1975's "Old Weird Harold" commercial. The little kid stares at the bowl of pudding and commands, "Old Weird Harold, you come out of there!" Helstein says it was the kid's spontaneous reaction to hearing Cosby go on about childhood friend Old Weird wanting to become a bowl of pudding.

In 1982's "Long Time Ago," Cosby takes up the defense of some kids who complain how infrequently they get Jell-O pudding—until, upon further probing, he discovers that their "long, long time ago" was actually just the night before.

Many of the pudding ads showed Cosby trying to persuade kids to give him some of their pudding, or leading them in call-and-response games as in 1977's "Neat-O."

Cosby began by telling the kids that his favorite childhood expression for anything good was neat-O.

"Like when the good guy would catch the bad guy and put him in jail I'd say—"

"Neat-O," the kids respond.

"Like when your mom makes you some Jell-O pudding," a kid jumps in.

"Neat-O," everyone shouts.

"So what do you think of Jell-O Pudding?" Cosby asks.

"Neat-O."

"What would you think if a dragon breathed fire on your toes?"

"Neat-O," they continue, now on a roll.

"Really?" Cosby asks. Realizing what they've done, the kids dissolve into giggles.

Cosby's ads for Jell-O gelatin have been faster paced and music driven. In 1994, he and some kids rapped about going "ape for the new Jell-O grape." "Jingle Bells" became "Jiggler Bells" in a tuneful 1992 holiday ad that ended with the jolly old elf catching Cosby about to eat his Jiggler treat.

As an adolescent, Cosby studied the way Ed Herlihy delivered recipe ads for *Kraft Television Theater*. Herlihy, Cosby once told *Newsweek* magazine, "could make pimento cheese on a slice of banana sound delicious." Cosby is proud of his own work for the same company, telling *Newsweek*, "I'm a damned fine pitch man."

A Jell-O pudding sales boost of 30 percent (by 1978) backs that statement up, as do celebrity likability and believability surveys, which Cosby consistently tops. (In one survey conducted by another Cosby client, the Ford Motor Company, only God and Walter Cronkite ranked higher.)

Cosby's credibility on Jell-O is rooted in personal experience dating back to his childhood.

"My parents were not poor, they were broke, and we ate Jell-O—gelatin, pudding, and tapioca," Cosby once said.

And now that he's among the wealthiest Americans, does he still eat it?

"Let's put it this way: they pay me pretty close to a million-something a year. Yes, I eat it," he told CNN's Jeanne Moos in 1997. His favorite flavor? Strawberry.

JELL-O Commercial Kids Do the Darndest Things

Cosby's Jell-O commercials are as much fun to make as they are to watch. At least that's how former Jell-O pudding kid Eugene Williams Jr. looks back on the experience. What he remembers about the Jell-O pudding commercial he did as a preschooler in the mid-'70s was "one kid who would not stop talking. So Cosby pushed some pudding up his nose. . . . We were laughing for most of the day," Williams said.

Cosby himself recalls the day a director interrupted shooting on one Jell-O commercial to ask a kid to eat the pudding while Cosby talked. "And the kid says, 'I don't like Jell-O pudding,'" Cosby said. "I just thought it was great that nobody checked . . . to see if the kid liked Jell-O pudding. Just set him down there 'cause he was great looking."

A more common problem occurs when the directors use that common phrase, "We're going to shoot that one more time."

"The kids write that down. If the director wants to do it again, they'll say, 'No, you said one more time,'" Cosby told the crowd at Jell-O's 100th birthday party in 1997.

Cosby says one of the biggest put-downs of his career came from one of the more cooperative pudding kids. After about twenty or thirty takes of the same bit, this kid asked Cosby if he did "this all the time." When he said yes, the kid said, "Then I'm going to college."

What's in Your Fridge?

University of Puget Sound college administrator Serni Solidarios has been rooting around this Jell-O mold of Bill Cosby's face to find the butter and pickles for the past twenty-three years. The mold was made by an art student at the school, who gave it to Cosby when he was performing on campus in 1978. After the show, Cosby told Solidarios, "I don't think I can take this on the plane. Can you keep it for me?" Solidarios said yes. And though the mold does not smell as sweetly as when he first put it in his refrigerator, Solidarios is a man of his word.

GOURMET GELATIN

Long a favorite at downscale and down-home restaurants, gelatin desserts began showing up on the menus of their upscale counterparts in the late 1990s in response to lighter eating and comfort food trends.

A berry gelatin dessert created by a pastry chef at the Four Seasons instigated a stampede at the extravagant fifty-two-dish buffet following the James Beard culinary awards in New York in May 1997.

"This is a revelation," Tim Zagat of restaurant guide fame told a reporter after downing three helpings of Bruno Feldeisen's Jiggling Fruit Mold with Berry Compote and Whipped Cream. (Total bill if Zagat had eaten the dessert at the Four Seasons' Fifty-Seven, Fifty-Seven Restaurant without accompanying drink: thirty dollars.)

Other gourmet chefs have joined in: Mary Brannigan at 27 Standard (mixed berries in a sauternes gelatin), Stephane Motir at the Tonic (terrine with muscat de Beaumes-de-Venise), and Eric Hebert at Jean Georges (chocolate and raspberry layered napoleon with strawberry Jello [*sic*] and vanilla ice cream), all of New York City; Andrew Marc Rothschild of The Marc in Chicago (apple grappa Jell-O) and Todd English at Julien in Boston (hot-and-cold citrus gelatin with Chiboust cream).

Most of these desserts were made with unflavored gelatin and fresh fruit. Some of the few exceptions were the gourmet gelatin creations of Scott Blackerby of Bambara in Salt Lake City, a place where real Jell-O is not only tolerated, it's celebrated. Here's a recipe for the upscale Jell-O Blackerby served to patrons of that New American bistro in the spring of 2000.

Mint Cream Dream

1 cup boiling water
1 (3-ounce) package lime Jell-O gelatin
3/4 cup sugar
Pinch of salt
1 cup cold water
1 cup whipping cream
3/4 teaspoon peppermint extract
Dark chocolate shavings (optional)

Stir boiling water into gelatin, sugar, and salt in large bowl at least 3 minutes until completely dissolved. Stir in cold water. Refrigerate until slightly thickened, about 10 minutes.

Beat whipping cream and peppermint extract with electric mixer on medium speed until soft peaks form. Gently stir into chilled gelatin until well blended.

Pour into molds or dessert glasses or into large glass dessert bowl. Refrigerate 3 hours or until set. Garnish with chocolate shavings, if desired. Serves 6.

JELL-O
Innovations

1969. Jell-O 1,2,3 is a science experiment disguised as dessert and one of Jell-O's most famous line extensions. After being whipped for four minutes and chilled for four hours, this uniquely self-disciplined product produces a dessert with a gelatin bottom, a chiffon middle, and a Cool Whip–like top. One magazine ad uses time-lapse photography to document the layer formation. Jell-O 1,2,3 sold like 1,2,3 initially but then quickly dropped off to next to nothing. Former Jell-O adman John Ferrell describes it as "a fad dessert. It was wonderful to watch— once."

Diet Jell-O is introduced and sold alongside its identical twin, D-Zerta, before consumers and Jell-O marketers notice the redundancy and it's discontinued.

1972. Jell-O Pastel, a gelatin dessert designed to be made with milk or cream instead of water, debuts then disappears. Could it be because consumers know regular Jell-O gelatin can also be made with milk? (Just let the hot water—gelatin mixture cool to room temperature before adding the milk.)

1974. Jell-O Instant Gelatin is introduced in test markets with the slogan, "Now it's never too late to make Jell-O." Advertisements claim the product sets in fifteen minutes alone, thirty minutes with fruit, or an hour in a mold. But one 1975 internal technical memo on the product reports, "A stable emulsion with Cool Whip was unattainable." No wonder it never goes national.

1975. Peach flavor returns.

1978. Apricot debuts and blackberry comes back.

1981. Jell-O is sold in a flexible serving recipe canister complete with measuring scoop, an idea that Jell-O Instant Pudding people copy with 1996's Stir 'n Snack. Kraft dessert marketing vice president Bob Lowe says the recipe canister failed because the real convenience issue with Jell-O is set time rather than package size.

Salad gelatins also reappear this year in selected markets in fruit flavor combinations. Package flags for the cooking impaired pair each flavor of Jell-O Flavor for Salads with pork, ham, poultry, or chicken. The problem, according to new product consultant Robert M. McMath, was that consumers who bought Jell-O Flavors for Salads had half as many occasions to make Jell-O as someone who bought regular Jell-O. So, in 1982, the salad flavors are tossed once again.

1984. General Foods builds on the huge success of its Jell-O Pudding Pops frozen pudding on a stick by introducing six flavors of frozen Jell-O Gelatin Pops. The introductory ad is a

---

Do-It-Yourself Self-Layering JELL-O

Kraft last sold the cult favorite **JELL-O 1,2,3** in 1996. Until it comes back, here's a way to make your own.

$^3/_4$ cup boiling water
1 (3-ounce) package Jell-O gelatin, any flavor
$^1/_2$ cup cold water
Ice cubes
$^1/_2$ cup whipped cream or Cool Whip

Pour boiling water into blender. Add gelatin. Cover and blend at low speed until gelatin is completely dissolved, about 30 seconds. Combine cold water and ice cubes to make 1 $^1/_4$ cups. Add to gelatin and stir until ice is partially melted. Then add whipped topping; blend at high speed for 30 seconds. Pour into dessert glasses. Chill about 30 minutes. Dessert layers as it chills. Serves 4.

Bill Cosby solo riff on how jealous his free hand is of the one holding the gelatin pop. The tag line is, "Real Jell-O gelatin. Only cooler." Jell-O Gelatin Pops disappear along with the pudding ones due to high production costs in 1993.

Jell-O formulates its diet gelatin with NutraSweet and relaunches it as Sugar Free Jell-O Gelatin. Initial ads show a diver jumping into the giant blue box as an unseen chorus urges, "Give in. Give in. Give in to the taste." These soon gave way to similarly hyperactive ads featuring island music and nautical settings as well as slower-paced female dieter testimonials to "the dessert you don't have to desert." Whether because of the ads or the diet-conscious times, Sugar Free Jell-O becomes one of the few unqualified Jell-O sales successes of the '80s.

1989. Boomer nostalgia for foods of their youth prompts a reintroduction of Jell-O 1,2,3. The cult favorite disappears again in 1996.

1991 to 1993. Ready-to-eat Jell-O Gelatin Snacks follow Jell-O Pudding Snacks into grocers' refrigerator cases over these two years as Jell-O attempts to meet the gelatin needs of an America too busy to wait around for its Jell-O to jell. It is so popular in its Denver test market that some stores find themselves restocking it three times a day. By September 1995, Jell-O's ready-to-eat gelatin sales are growing by as much as 11 percent a year. (Although costs are high compared to their boxed products, Kraft dares not abandon a product this popular, especially not since ConAgra moved in with its Jolly Rancher Gel Snacks.)

1992. Berry blue Jell-O is introduced by a blues-singing Bill Cosby and becomes Jell-O's third most popular color (after red and orange). Kids like the shock value of eating something that looks like congealed

Windex. The similarly kid-friendly watermelon and grape follow in 1993 and 1994, respectively.

1994. Ready-to-eat refrigerated Sugar Free Jell-O Gelatin Snacks debut. Today 40 percent of all Jell-O gelatin sold is sugar free, and 45 percent of all those sales is to diabetics.

After almost 100 years of making do with other red flavors, Thanksgiving mold makers are finally graced with cranberry-flavored Jell-O. Sugar free cranberry, cranberry strawberry, and cranberry raspberry blends follow in 1995.

1995. The marriage of Kraft and General Foods turns Kraft's Light 'n Lively Kid Pack Yogurt into Jell-O Kid Pack Yogurt. Within six months the yogurt is topped with a plastic dome of tiny Jell-O Jigglers and the product is called Jell-O Jigglers Bits & Yogurt. A kids' yogurt with a gelatin texture called Jell-O Wiggle is also tried but never gets out of northeastern test markets.

1996. The Jell-O package is temporarily redesigned to feature characters from the Mighty Morphin Power Rangers—the black ranger prompting a black Jell-O flavored like blackberries. The brand also forges brief marketing alliances with *Jurassic Park*, Peanuts, Furby, the Flintstones, and NASCAR racing.

Jell-O targets America's growing Hispanic population with new tropical blend flavors including peach passion fruit and island pineapple.

1997. Jell-O celebrates its 100th birthday by introducing a limited-edition sparkling white grape flavor, designed to be made with a carbonated beverage and dubbed "The Champagne of Jell-O." Despite one critic's assertion that "that's like calling Spam the filet mignon of meats," sales are so sparkling that white grape becomes the start of a new sub-line of special occasion Jell-Os, which by 1999 also includes sparkling wild berry and sparkling mandarin orange.

JELL-O Slogans

1970 If it was there you'd eat it
1970 Put a Jell-O out tonight
1971 Tastes as good as it wobbles
1971 The light snack
1971 The only snack that can fit the bill without filling you up
1971 Somehow it's always right
1972 Make someone happy. Make someone Jell-O.
1973 It's almost as easy as Jell-O
1973 Start with Jell-O gelatin
1975 Don't say no, say Jell-O
1978 Jell-O is thrilling but not filling
1979 We got the fruit so you could get the taste
1979 Make some fun
1983 Make it Jell-O. Create a sensation.
1984 Give in to the taste
1985 We're up to something good
1986 We've got fruit appeal
1987 The dessert you won't have to desert
1987 The quickest way to find a smile
1987 What being a kid is all about
1988 You can't be a kid without it
1990 Jell-O gelatin's place is a kid's face
1992 Have your fun and eat it too
1995 Still the coolest
1995 It's alive
1998 Smile more
1999 Juice up your Jell-O
2000 I could go for something Jell-O
2001 Make some magic

Put a Jell-O out tonight.

NET WT OZ (85g)

THE HOUSE THAT JELL-O BUILT

Chapter 6

MAKING JELL-O

*C*ompared to making commercial quantities of soup, sausage, or even brownies, making Jell-O gelatin is pure simplicity. If you've ever followed a recipe calling for a packet of unflavored gelatin, sugar, and fruit, you know what we mean. Kraft follows essentially the same recipe in the Jell-O area of its Dover, Delaware, plant except for quantities that yield three million servings per day versus the four to six servings you might make in your own home.

Nowadays 90 percent of all dry packaged American Jell-O is made in Dover. The remaining 10 percent (mostly the less popular flavors) are made in San Leandro, California. Ready-to-eat Jell-O is made in the Kraft facility in Mason City, Iowa. Jell-O is also made in Mexico and Canada for sale in those countries. (The Product of Canada statement you may see on full-sugar boxes of Jell-O is due to ingredients that come from our neighbor to the north. But rest assured that all U.S.-sold packages of this American food icon are still made and boxed in America.)

A Sweet Setting

Early Jell-O was made in LeRoy, New York, in an ivy-covered brick factory building that advertising materials described in idyllic terms. "On all fall and winter days log-fires burn cheerfully in the offices of the executives. In spring and summer many kinds of birds . . . flit gaily about the lawn." As for the Jell-O employees, they are "immaculate" and "all Americans. Strikes or labor troubles do not occur . . . Their work reminds one of a big sociable sort of jelling-bee."

Indeed, ninety-nine-year-old retiree Catherine Powers, who joined the company after being orphaned at age thirteen, remembers how her fellow recipe book inserters covered for her until she got up to speed. Frances Riggi's husband was convalescing from a bad accident and the family was almost without food the day she received the phone call offering her a job at the Jell-O plant—even though she had never applied for work there.

That kind of big business paternalism toward this small town ended in March 1962

when Jell-O owner General Foods announced that it was going to consolidate four northeastern factories—including Jell-O—into one central but as yet undetermined location. One town tried to woo General Foods by skywriting "We want Jell-O" over corporate headquarters; another, by having three thousand of its residents send letters and box tops from General Foods products. But in the end, they settled on tax-friendly Dover, Delaware, where Jell-O production takes up two acres of a twenty-seven-acre facility that also supplies America with Minute Rice, Baker's Coconut, Stove Top Stuffing, Shake and Bake, Dream Whip, Kool-Aid, Country Time Lemonade, and Tang.

Secret Process

In most ways, Jell-O making has changed very little since its earliest days. Jell-O still has a vertical-manufacturing setup, for instance. The biggest differences are in the ingredients, the increased sophistication of the machinery, and the size and secrecy of the operation. The Jell-O factory in LeRoy offered public plant tours. But Central Delaware Chamber of Commerce vice president Allen S. Hedgecock says it's easier to get into Dover Air Force Base than the Kraft plant in Dover. The company doesn't even give a Jell-O biographer a tour or plant pictures, leaving her to glean details of contemporary production from plant materials manager Connie Longshore.

Strong Fingernails? Lush Locks? Straight Talk about Gelatin Nutrition

Jell-O is now served in hospitals under that well-worn medical rule, "do no harm."

But can eating gelatin do you any good? The question has been a matter of debate over the decades—and centuries.

In the eighteenth century people believed that meat's nutritive values actually flowed out in the form of gelatin. A similar view held sway in nineteenth-century France when endorsement by the Academy of Medicine of Paris led to gelatin's widespread use in hospitals.

Gelatin's nutritional reputation suffered a setback in the mid-1800s when some dogs used in an experiment conducted by France's second gelatin commission turned up their noses at the stuff but that was only because "the commission . . . thought a substance refused by an animal because of its taste could not have food value," a March 1916 edition of *Scientific American* noted. "Moreover," the magazine continued with its twentieth-century hindsight, "these creatures were kept in cages in a cellar" and served plain dry gelatin rather than the more appetizing jellied kind. But gelatin was back in favor by 1870, when gelatin was served to commoners during the siege of Paris.

A Jell-O institutional ad from the '20s reported that some physicians were studying "the value of feeding [Jell-O] to patients prior to tonsillectomy and other surgical operations in order to increase the coagulability of the blood . . . Some physicians believe that it also tends to reduce hemorrhage after childbirth."

In the late '30s, news of a study proving gelatin to be a muscle stimulant caused a run on Knox Gelatine.

Claims that gelatin promotes fingernail and hair growth and strength first appeared in the '50s and continue to this day although the studies are controversial. They also don't make a lot of sense in light of modern understanding about human nutrition.

Today nutritionists believe gelatin is missing two amino acids needed for its protein to be utilized for human cell growth. Therefore it is simply burned up as calories. (Since gelatin's two missing amino acids are in milk products, some theorize that topping your Jell-O with cream or milk will allow your body to realize the nutritional advantages of gelatin's protein—although no one seems sure how much milk or cream you'd need to eat, or when, to make this happen.) The Jell-O box's own nutrition facts panel says that its two grams of protein are "not a significant source of protein."

Recent studies on gelatin's value in reducing joint pain and stiffness in athletes and arthritis sufferers show promise (perhaps because gelatin is made from cartilage, among other collagen-containing animal parts). But large amounts of gelatin are required. And given the history of changing opinion about gelatin nutrition, we wouldn't throw out our Bengay just yet.

GIRLS WANTED

We offer steady employ-
ment to girls and women,
light work in factory, good
wages. Either write or apply
in person at our office.

The Genesee Pure Food Co.

According to Longshore, Jell-O production begins on the Dover plant's fourth floor where the ingredients to make Jell-O are brought in and stored. First and foremost is sugar, since it accounts for more than 80 percent of Jell-O in the package (but only 14 percent after it's prepared with the standard two cups of water). Sugar was originally delivered in barrels (up to 22,000 at the LeRoy plant in 1921) but now it is stored in 300,000-pound silos.

"From Cuba, Porto [*sic*] Rico, and Java comes the pure cane sugar that contributes its highly nutritious elements to Jell-O," intoned one promotional piece from 1931, when sugar was apparently thought to have some nutrition. In the

Barrels of sugar stored at the original factory

'50s, the company boasted of daily using twice the sugar consumed by the nearby city of Rochester.

Skating on Gelatin

Next come sacks of powdered gelatin, described in a 1923 house ad as being "as pure and clean a product as

Do-It-Yourself JELL-O

The same basic steps involved in making Jell-O in the giant Kraft plant can be replicated on a much smaller scale to make custom flavored gelatin dishes in your own home. The liquid could be tea, coffee, juice, wine, water, soda, or juice concentrate (reconstituted with somewhat less water than usual), or any combination of liquids that appeals.

Food coloring and common flavor extracts (such as root beer, vanilla, almond, and mint) can be purchased in the baking aisle of any supermarket, and many other extract flavors are available from beer- and wine-making stores.

1 envelope (1 tablespoon) Knox or other unflavored gelatin powder
1/2 cup cold liquid
Up to 1/4 cup sugar (optional)
1 1/2 cups liquid, heated to boiling
Flavor extract and/or spices, to taste (optional)
Food coloring, for looks (optional)
Up to 1 1/2 cups fruit, vegetables, candy, or whatever (optional)

In medium bowl, sprinkle unflavored gelatin over cold liquid; let stand 1 minute. Add sugar (if you're making a dessert-style dish and the liquid isn't already sweet) and hot liquid, and stir until gelatin is completely dissolved, about 5 minutes. Stir in extract, spices, and coloring, if using.

If adding solids, chill gelatin in mixing bowl until it is the consistency of unbeaten egg whites (about 40 minutes) before folding them in. Then pour into serving dishes and refrigerate another 2 1/2 hours.

If not adding solids, just pour into mold or dishes and chill about 3 hours, or until firm. Serves 4 adventurous souls.

the choicest chops or steaks that ever came out of a modern packing plant," a curious analogy that would never be allowed today due to widespread squeamishness about any foods with animal origins. The gelatin then came from France, Germany, and "spick-and-span little Holland" as well as domestic sources. Today it all comes from General Foods' own suburban Boston Atlantic Gelatin plant, which is indirectly responsible for that Nancy Kerrigan–Tonya Harding knee-knocking incident (since Kerrigan's ice-skating lessons were partially funded by her father's Atlantic Gelatin welding job) and more directly responsible for certain not-so-sweet smells that have been the subject of numerous citizen complaints and local newspaper stories. If Kraft executives are tight-lipped about production at Dover, they are closemouthed about Atlantic Gelatin despite its crucial contribution to Jell-O's wiggle. Without gelatin, Jell-O would merely be Kool-Aid.

Fruit Appeal

Completing the Jell-O ingredient list are colors and flavors and acids that fine-tune the flavors. Originally they were all natural extracts from fruits and herbs and the inspiration for some fairly rhapsodic advertising pieces.

"In the sun-ripened vineyards of France and Italy, laughing peasant girls pluck wine grapes from heavily burdened vines. From the juice of these grapes . . . comes tartaric acid . . . See the curious oxcarts of Canary and Cape Verde, and caravans crossing India, bearing the rare raw materials that impart the brilliant edible coloring. . . . Behold Sicily's sun-drenched orange and lemon groves, Brazil's chocolate lands," and America's own "bursting-ripe fat berries . . . all contributing their share to the natural fruit flavors that permeate this wholesome dessert."

Jell-O never did own any of its own fruit fields although for years visitors to the LeRoy plant asked to see them. The fruits came to LeRoy as jugs of concentrated oil essences, which a worker in a 1921 plant tour booklet was shown mixing in flasks like some Dr. Fruitenstein. Today only the citrus flavors have any natural flavors.

The Jell-O laboratory

Gelatin Making: The Unprettified Story

Big Boy hamburgers come from slaughterhouses. Sheep gut makes violins sing. Someday we'll all die. When you really look closely enough, nothing is pretty—gaily colored Jell-O gelatin molds included.

That's because the gelatin that makes Jell-O so jolly jiggly is basically boiled Bessie and Porky Pig. To put it more precisely, it's the bones, skins, and hides of Bessie and Porky that are boiled for the gelatin their protein-rich collagen—the fibrous part of skin, tendons, ligaments, and bones—will yield. If you've ever boiled meat bones to make soup then put it in the refrigerator, you've probably noticed the jellylike film that forms on top. That's gelatin making in miniature.

A '20s recipe booklet entitled *Jell-O: Of What and How Made* tried to put a good face on large-scale gelatin making, calling gelatin the "'rock crystal' of the animal kingdom" and describing the process this way. "Starting from the cartilaginous parts, this pure food product is obtained by a long series of boilings and filterings in the form of a delicate, colorless and transparent jelly from which every trace of grossness has been removed . . ."

To get a little more gross about it, commercial gelatin makers begin by grinding up bones and cutting up skin and hides obtained from slaughterhouses, meat packers, and tanneries (if properly pretreated, even shoes and purses can be recycled into dessert!). After washing, these materials are soaked in acid and/or lime, then washed again until all the fat, hair, skin, and other nongelatin stuff has either disintegrated or floated away in wastewater that, on a hot day . . . well, let's just say P.U.

It's the next step—boiling—that actually renders the gelatin, which is then concentrated, filtered, and cooled to form gelatinous sheets. Once dried, it is ground to a powder and then blended with other batches to create a gelatin of the correct purity and strength to meet its intended use.

About 245,000 tons of gelatin are produced more or less like this worldwide each year, 65 percent of which end up being consumed, most commonly in gelatin salads or desserts but also in candy (especially the gummy kinds) and in ice cream and yogurt (where it serves as a stabilizer). The majority of the remaining 35 percent is used to make gel-cap pills and surgical dressings that literally melt away; the rest to make photographic paper and film. It's also used to make glue (just as it was in Peter Cooper's time).

Gelatin concentrate

Extruding through rotator

Gelatin drying before being milled

Jelly Making: A Gonzo Father's Account

Ralph Steadman offered an alternative view of Jell-O making in 1967's *Jelly Book*—jelly being the name for flavored gelatin in England, where the illustrator and writer lives.

Steadman is probably best known for his collaborations with "gonzo" journalist Hunter S. Thompson and his collections of caustic political satire, *America* and *Scar Strangled Banger*. (In the latter, Steadman depicts former president Gerald Ford as the monster creation of a Dr. Frankenstein–like Henry Kissinger.) But *Ralph Steadman's Jelly Book* is a cheery and imaginative delight.

That's because Steadman wrote it for his two-and-a-half-year-old daughter, Genevieve, when she was hospitalized over the holidays for a serious intestinal problem. To help cheer her up, Steadman decorated her hospital ward with pictures of the one food she and the other sick children were able to eat. He only put words to the pictures later when his publisher was looking for a new book.

Those words tell of a land where jelly literally grows on trees. After picking, it is flown by elephants to the factory where the good jelly is separated from the bad. The bad jelly is used to stuff pillows and mattresses; the good is mixed by batting it about a tennis court. Then it's squashed into lumps by a jelly squasher named Barry and put into boxes that are stacked on cows' heads.

Why cows?

Because cows can provide the cream that tastes so good with jelly. Then the cows are herded into a plane (most go up front because, Steadman notes, "Cows always like to ride up front near the pilot") and flown to a faraway city where their plane is met by the mayor. The cows process around the streets of the city to cheering crowds. The parade—and also the book—ends with a big party where everyone eats jelly.

There's also a happy ending to the story behind the story. Little Genevieve did recover from her illness and now exercises the family artistic genes designing shoes.

The switch to the less costly artificial colors, artificial flavors and acids, and acid buffers now used began in the late '30s. In the early '40s, Jack Benny show announcer Don Wilson crowed about raspberry Jell-O's new "better than ever" flavor, obtained by its new "artificially enhanced" natural flavor base. In the techno-obsessed '50s, the word "imitation" became a prominent part of new flavor names.

Today fifty-pound boxes of the colors and flavors join Jell-O's other ingredients in a pipe or conveyor ride down to the third floor, where they're weighed, then dumped into bins that ride a rail down to the second-floor mixing room. All these ingredients then go into thirty-six-hundred-pound mixers, along with the occasional sack or two of so-called minor flavoring or coloring.

Setting the Schedule

Which flavors they make on any one day depends on where they are in the one-and-a-half to two-week Jell-O flavor-making rotation that starts with the lightest colors, like white grape and lemon (to minimize equipment cleanup). Flavor production is determined by demand: a popular flavor like strawberry could run two full days on a single machine; orange-pineapple may only require half a shift.

In pre–Environmental Protection Agency days, townspeople could identify the flavor of the day by checking the color of the creek that ran behind the LeRoy plant. It usually ran red, the color of the most popular flavors. Years after Jell-O had left LeRoy, the repainted walls in the old Jell-O plant still leached red.

Now as then, the Jell-O ingredients are blended for only minutes before the bottoms of the mixers yawn open and the Jell-O powder falls down a feeder to the first-floor packaging line.

Until 1914, all the packages were made and filled by hand by women dressed in nurselike whites. The glassine inner bags were formed and glued over

wooden blocks, and often cracked, letting moisture in and causing the powder to cake. They were filled the same way a home cook would measure off a cup of flour: by dipping a measuring spoon into a receptacle of Jell-O powder, then leveling it off with a stick. These same crews of women glued the Jell-O cartons. As Jell-O sales increased, recruiting for these ten-cent-an-hour jobs widened to surrounding towns, and coaches were added to the trains from the neighboring city of Batavia to accommodate the new workers.

The labor and product-caking problems both ended in 1914 when Andrew Nico (still hard at work after turning down the chance to buy Jell-O for thirty-five dollars many years before) and Otis E.

Glidden (a Jell-O salesman who went on to found his own competing Jiffy-Jell brand gelatin) invented the seamless, sealed waxed-paper bag. In December 1950, *Modern Packaging* magazine nominated Jell-O for its Hall of Fame largely because of the then thirty-six-year-old bag, which "has become the basic pattern for high-speed, economical packaging of practically every similar product on the market." (This followed an earlier All-American Package Competition Award Jell-O had received from the same magazine for its pioneering efforts printing cartons using photographic plates.)

Besides preventing caking, the seamless package gave Jell-O the extended shelf life it needed for full national distribution. And it could be made by machine. The proud company displayed one of these new Anderson packaging machines at the 1915 Panama Exposition in San Francisco, and featured pictures of it and the bags it made in advertising and recipe booklets through the '20s. A Jell-O recipe booklet with the awkward title "*Of What and How Made*" explained how the machines "measure an exact amount of Jell-O, make a moisture-proof bag, fill the bag with Jell-O, seal the bag against air and moisture, open a carton, place the bag and a recipe in the carton, glue the carton and pass the completed package to [an] operator. *All in two seconds*," ending in italics for emphasis. A 1921 plant tour booklet enthused of the Anderson, "This machine does everything but talk!"

By the mid-'20s, forty-two of these machines were spitting out thirty Jell-O boxes a minute each in LeRoy. The packaging machines in use in the '50s could produce eighty-five filled boxes per minute; ones from the early '60s, three hundred per minute or half the capacity of those currently in use at Dover.

After being glued shut and weighed, each Jell-O box is stamped with a code that is the food product equivalent of a birth certificate. Jell-O box codes feature the last digit of the year it was made, the day of the year (ranging from 1, for January 1, to 365), a plant letter, the production line number, and the moment the box was produced in twenty-four-hour, or military, time. A Jell-O box stamped 1030D6 08:59, for instance, came off Jell-O production line 6 in Dover at 8:59 A.M. on January 30, 2001.

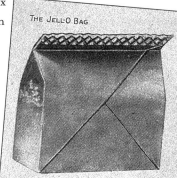

THE JELL-O BAG

This JELL-O SAFETY BAG protects Jell-O inside the carton.

Being air-tight it keeps the flavor at full strength.

The Safety Bag, made of Waxed Paper and hermetically sealed, affords absolute protection to the Jell-O inside. Moisture is kept out and the flavor is kept in. Jell-O so protected will remain for years as pure and sweet as on the day it was made.

This is the JELL-O PACKAGE complete

The Safety Bag is inside. Jell-O is never sold in any other kind of package.

CANADA'S MOST FAMOUS DESSERT

JELL-O

TRADE MARK REG. CAN. PAT. OFF.
A JELLY POWDER

DELICATE DELIGHTFUL DAINTY

STRAWBERRY

PURE FRUIT FLAVOR
VEGETABLE COLOR
THE GENESEE PURE FOOD CO. OF CANADA, LIMITED
BRIDGEBURG, ONT.

JELL-O Science 101

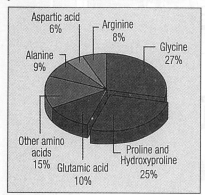

- Aspartic acid 6%
- Arginine 8%
- Glycine 27%
- Alanine 9%
- Other amino acids 15%
- Glutamic acid 10%
- Proline and Hydroxyproline 25%

OK kids, listen up: Today's lesson is about the science behind Jell-O gelatin's strange behavior.

Gelatin is composed of protein molecules, which are themselves constructed of eighteen amino acids lined together in three helical chains. You remember helical chains—they were what Watson and Crick studied when they were trying to come up with the structure of DNA. But did you know that the pair actually began their study of protein structure on gelatin from Atlantic Gelatin—the same plant that is still the source of all the gelatin in Jell-O?

When the gelatin protein chains are placed in hot water (as when you pour a box of Jell-O into a cup of hot water), they separate. When the water-gelatin mixture cools in your refrigerator, the gelatin protein chains re-form—but less securely than before because of the water molecules trapped in between the chains. That water is what makes Jell-O wiggle.

If you've ever made the mistake of trying to loosen a gelatin mold by placing it in hot (instead of lukewarm) water, you also know that gelatin is thermoreversible. Warm it up and it will turn back into a liquid, until it cools down and forms gelatin again—so on, ad infinitum—or almost as long as the school day.

The gelatin protein chain can also be broken down by enzymes found in fresh or frozen pineapple, kiwi, figs, gingerroot, guava, and papaya. That's why Jell-O warns consumers against using these products in Jell-O recipes unless they're canned or cooked. (Heat used in canning kills the enzymes.)

Adding fruit to Jell-O is a lesson in density. Canned fruits packed in heavy syrup and seedless grapes will sink in newly dissolved Jell-O because they are denser (have more mass per volume) than Jell-O liquid. But less dense fresh produce such as diced apples, sliced bananas, orange sections, strawberries, shredded carrots, sliced cucumbers, and celery—not to mention marshmallows and chopped nuts—will all float. People who want their add-ins to set throughout their mold rather than on the bottom or the top need to stir them in after the protein chains of Jell-O have re-formed with water.

Anyone who doesn't know what that means needs to go home and study their notes from today.

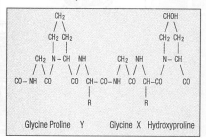

Packing the Powder

Finally, the Jell-O boxes are packaged for shipping. Originally they were put in finger-lapped wooden crates that not only protected the merchandise, but were themselves prized by consumers who turned them into wheelbarrows, fishing tackle boxes, even radio cases. The company eventually switched to the cheaper cardboard and now merely bundles the twenty-four boxes in brown paper.

These bundles normally sit in the factory at least a

day, or more than long enough to spot problems before shipping. Tests for color, flavor, texture, and acidity occur along the line and also in a laboratory that includes a library of Jell-O samples going back two years. In 1937, one laboratory job was devoted exclusively to clocking Jell-O's setting time. All production would stop while one woman dissolved a small amount of Jell-O powder in a test tube and placed it in a rack of ice water while the production employee who had delivered the sample waited. Jell-O's bloom strength, or bounciness (to put it nontechnically), is checked by a machine called a gelometer. It consists of a plunger and equipment

The Jell-O Packing Machine

to measure its movement. Bloom strength is the force (recorded in grams) required for a plunger to make set gelatin move 4 millimeters. Generally gelatin desserts must be at least 220 grams strong.

If all goes well, the 60 people who now make Jell-O at Dover can go home knowing the world is 750,000 boxes bouncier thanks to their efforts that day. Should they ever forget, they are reminded when they take a shower and the rinse water runs Jell-O red.

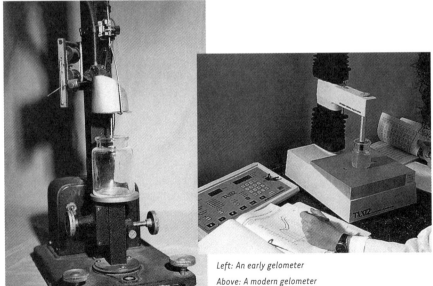

Left: An early gelometer
Above: A modern gelometer

Kosher JELL-O: The Pigskin Paradox

Rabbis visit Atlantic Gelatin.

People who keep kosher can't eat pig.

Pigskins are often used to make the gelatin in Jell-O.

And yet the little *K* near the serving-size information on the Jell-O box indicates that Jell-O is kosher.

How can this be?

It's because there's no single known authority or widely accepted standards behind the *K* designation Jell-O bears.

Most kosher symbols on food packages are trademarked by certifying organizations that stand behind the validity of the designation. For instance, a *U* within a circle on a food product denotes the blessing of the Union of Orthodox Jewish Congregations of America, a nonprofit agency that certifies a majority of America's kosher foods. But the plain, untrademarked *K* on the Jell-O package might mean nothing more than that a manufacturer believes its product is kosher.

Kraft actually does have its Atlantic Gelatin plant inspected by rabbis, including Rabbis Yehuda Gershuni and Jehiel M. Goldsmith, whose official statement on "The Halachic Basis of our Kashruth Certification of Atlantic Gelatin and the General Foods Products containing this Gelatin" argues that the chemical solutions used to render gelatin from pork skins transforms the pork into an entirely different foodstuff.

Citing such authorities as the Shulchan Aruch, Rama, Schach (whoever or whatever they are), and quoting the Ritvo that preceded them, Gershuni and Goldsmith write, "Where [a food article] becomes inedible even for a dog, although it is later made edible, it cannot again assume an 'issur' [prohibition]."

Some text on the reverse side of this official "responsum"—presumably written by someone at Kraft—notes the U.S. government's seeming concurrence with this argument, since gelatin products are regulated by the Food and Drug Administration rather than the meat-inspecting Department of Agriculture.

This explanation is probably good enough for the increasing numbers of non-Jews who buy kosher products out of a general sense that they are better for you or even for some liberal Reform or Conservative Jews—but not for serious kosher consumers.

Joe M. Regenstein of the Cornell Kosher Food Initiative, a program to promote understanding between the food industry, the religious supervisory agencies, and the public, will say only that Kraft is "way out of the mainstream on their view of gelatin" and probably realizes it, judging from a company-generated list of Kraft kosher products he once saw that was notably missing the name of their most important prepared dessert.

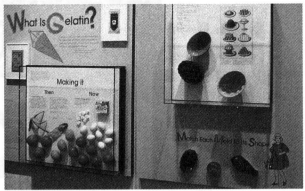

Exhibits at the Jell-O museum

Chapter 7

CELEBRATING JELL-O

*J*ell-O gelatin dishes are quickly consumed. Jell-O advertising campaigns change. Consumers' interest can be fleeting.

So what the heck can Jell-O aficionados count on? Gelatinously speaking, what's important? What lasts?

The following are seminal events and pivotal people and places in the life of Jell-O. Some of these pillars of Jell-O history and culture are still with us; some are long gone. But if you want to consider yourself well informed about Jell-O culture, you must read on.

The Museum

Although more popularly known as the Jell-O museum, the real name of the world's only collection of gelatin artifacts and facts open to the public is the Jell-O Gallery—for good reason. The nineteen oil paintings they own that were used to illustrate early Jell-O ads and recipe booklets will be the highlight of any visit to this museum in Jell-O's birthplace of LeRoy, New York.

Though the Jell-O museum doesn't own any artwork by Rose O'Neill, Norman Rockwell, or Maxfield Parrish, it does have interesting pictures of an Eskimo dad bringing home a crate of Jell-O to his delighted family, the critical moment of Jell-O unmolding,

The author

and gorgeous Jell-O still lifes. Every fine-art student in America should be required to study Guy Rowe's masterful capturing of Jell-O gelatin's translucence, for instance.

These paintings line the walls of a presentation of Jell-O legend and lore far slicker than you'd expect from a historical society the size of LeRoy's. That's because the core of the exhibit was actually created as a temporary hallway installation at Rochester's much larger Strong Museum in 1993. In its current permanent incarnation in the former LeRoy High School, a stone building set back behind the historical society's headquarters and linked to Main Street by the Jell-O Brick Road, the Jell-O Gallery Exhibit is half hands-on children's museum and half grown-up-oriented explication of how this strange stuff came be such a popular dessert.

Visitors get to see the instrument used to ensure each batch of gelatin has its proper bounce (called a gelometer), view near-identical brain and gelatin mold EEG readings from a local hospital, and contribute to a visitor comment book filled with accounts of Jell-O school cafeteria high jinks.

Children and adults alike should enjoy posing for pictures in the wooden Jell-O delivery truck and Jell-O Girl cutouts.

The Jell-O Gallery gift shop's extensive offerings include Jell-O still life pins (complete with tiny frames), mugs, rulers, refrigerator magnets, coloring books, T-shirts—in short, almost everything that you can think of except the actual Jell-O on the minds of everyone walking out of here.

The Historian

When Jell-O was made in LeRoy, there was never any need for residents to buy it in a store. (It walked out the

Lynne Belluscio

factory door.) After General Foods left town in 1964, many LeRoyans swore they'd never buy it. That might be the situation still but for the diplomatic efforts of town historical society director Lynne Belluscio.

It was the hardworking, fast-talking Belluscio who convinced organizers of the town's annual summer Oatka Festival to make the 1997 event into a celebration of Jell-O gelatin's 100th birthday. She was also the person who sweet-talked Kraft out of the fifty thousand dollars needed to

JELL-O
Horseradish Relish

Lynne Belluscio first made this 1937 Jell-O recipe booklet offering for an edible Jell-O exhibit she staged at the LeRoy Historical Society in 1992. It's now one of her favorite Jell-O recipes. "It's a real sleeper," she insists.

1 green bell pepper
1 (3-ounce) package lemon Jell-O gelatin
2 cups boiling water
2 tablespoons white vinegar
1 (4-ounce) jar chopped pimento, drained
1/2 cup horseradish

Thinly slice half the green pepper into rings; finely chop the other half. In a small bowl combine the Jell-O with the water and vinegar. Stir until Jell-O dissolves completely. Add the pimento, chopped green pepper, and horseradish. Cool to room temperature. Pour into 4- to 6-cup mold. Refrigerate about an hour or until it begins to thicken. Then place pepper rings inside the mold in an attractive way. Return to refrigerator until set. Unmold and serve in slices.

turn the old LeRoy High School into the permanent home for the Jell-O exhibit she curated at the Strong Museum in Rochester (and several years later, got them to ante up another fifty thousand dollars for renovations that included up-to-code bathrooms).

Belluscio traces her fondness for Jell-O back to church potlucks of her Rochester youth, when it was a safe haven in a sea of unidentifiable casseroles. "I always liked knowing the food I was eating. With Jell-O you could always see what you were getting."

Since becoming director of the LeRoy Historical Society in 1988, Belluscio has written lengthy articles for the local weekly newspaper detailing the final disposition of a chair that Jell-O heir Donald Woodward put into one of Amelia Earhart's old planes and speculating whether the name of the high school football team had been inspired by a Jell-O ad. She regularly fields questions from Jell-O collectors and corresponds with little old ladies who write to the old Jell-O factory for fifty-year-old mold premiums. Even Jell-O's public relations agency defers to her on matters of Jell-O history.

That's why Belluscio is just as likely to be lecturing Smithsonian historians about the dangers of picking a bright color of Jell-O for wrestling ("Your body will turn that color," she warned them in 1991) and trying to stump the panel about her wacky historical subspecialty on the game show revival *To Tell the Truth*, as cataloging donations and organizing exhibits for the historical society.

"When I was planning my life's goals, it never entered my mind that I would someday be talking about weird Jell-O with Brother Weeze," wrote Belluscio of her conversation with a local radio personality. Now, it's harder to imagine her in a room of musty old books. This is a woman who once talked a local hospital into performing an EEG on a bowl of Jell-O as a publicity stunt, and who shows up at museum conferences bearing a pan full of Jell-O shots and wearing earrings fashioned from mini tin molds.

Belluscio's Jell-O activity has increased visibility for

a town previously renowned mainly as the birthplace of the stringless string bean. Visits to the historical society alone have increased from one bus tour a year pre–Jell-O Gallery to sixty in 2000. But town leaders have drawn the line at Belluscio's idea of turning their annual summer Oatka Festival into an annual Jell-O Jubilee.

"I told them that it could be a national festival in five years," says Belluscio. But they told her there was no room for Jell-O in a festival celebrating contemporary LeRoy.

The Conference

Most days Smithsonian Institution employees are able to take their jobs as stewards of American history seriously. But on April Fool's Day, 1991, employees of the National Museum of American History's Department of the History of Science and Technology let loose a little.

The morning session of the First Annual Smithsonian Conference on Jell-O History mocked an academic conference and featured Jell-O mold-adorned name badges and paper presentations that ranged from the mostly serious to the wholly fanciful. The former included LeRoy town historian Lynne Belluscio's story of Jell-O's invention and Smithsonian staffer Roger White's account of the rise of Jack Benny's Jell-O-sponsored radio show; the latter, retired Division of Transportation employee Jack White's look at Jell-O's prehistoric origins (basically dinosaur hooves fell into a geyser, and Jell-O popped out).

In a similar vein was Rayna Green's "White Religious Cults: Lime Jell-O and Little Marshmallows."

"I have come before you today with a report on a long-term ethnographic study of white people's culture undertaken by a team of distinguished Indian anthropologists, archaeologists and psychologists, ethnologists and priests who've been excavating several sites of primary importance to white culture in its apex, i.e., circa 1950s," Green began in her best mock academic snooty tone.

Their findings? Jell-O with little marshmallows was a ritual food prepared according to instructions from religious tracts such as *Woman's Day*, *Today's Home*, and *House Beautiful*, and frequently served "in association with such other holy foods as iceberg lettuce, white bread, and mayonnaise."

Among the actual facts presented during the morning session:

A 1905 treatise on gelatin-making recommended using calves' feet and waste from button makers. Upper thighbones are not advised "as they can be more advantageously used for the manufacture of piano keys and the handles of tooth-brushes" (from Peter Liebhold's "Gelatin Before Jell-O" talk).

The National Museum of American History's cafeteria typically sells about 170 cups of Jell-O a week. (And 126 boxes of Jell-O were sold in supermarkets across America in the time it took presenter Betsy Burstein to say that.)

In 1945, U.S. government specifications for gelatin limited its bacterial count to no more than five thousand per gram. University of Maryland history professor Robert Friedel also showed the crowd a

Periodic Table of the Really Important Elements, which included Jell-O (Je), Hydrox (Hy), and WD-40 (Wd).

Generally speaking, research methods employed by the Jell-O scholars were reminiscent of those used by junior high school students faced with a term paper the same night their favorite TV show was on.

Smithsonian historian Karen Linn researched the great debate over whether Jell-O is salad or dessert by talking to her parents (who ate it as part of the main meal) and her in-laws (who ate it only for dessert). Another speaker cited the Jell-O 800 number as a primary source.

The afternoon was devoted to demonstrations and the Jell-Off Cook-Off (itself a spin-off of the museum Department of Conservation's annual bake-off). Demonstrator Nanci Edwards appeared in chef's whites adorned by a Jell-O box to successfully separate Jell-O from its mold to thunderous applause.

Attendees paid one dollar to taste Jell-Off entries that included vodka Jell-O cubes, Jell-O bread, Primordial Aspic (gummy worms and fish swimming in green Jell-O), and undescended Twinkies floating in orange Jell-O.

Entrants had been told their work would be judged by the following criteria: taste, level of disgust, jiggle, political correctness, aesthetics (including suspension of objects and disbelief), volatility, and long-term stability. But the judges pretty much did what they wanted.

For instance, a raspberry chicken with hatching eggs received a first prize for being most disgusting and politically incorrect. A creation called Grapes in

Suspension was honored for being the dessert your grandmother would most like you to bring to her house. Best in show went to a pastel Jell-O rainbow cake, mainly because, judge foreman Art Molella explained, "We couldn't come to any consensus and the two people who were the loudest wanted it."

Winners received packets of gelatin with which "to continue their good work" —although there never was a Second Annual Conference on Jell-O. Instead the April 1 conference was redubbed the Annual (Usually) Conference on Stuff and has gone on to examine peanut butter, corn, pie, and, in 1994, Rayna Green's marshmallows.

The Art Show

Carla Zimmerman blames it on the Pacific Northwest's long winters. After five months of wet and gray, people start to go a little crazy, the art gallery curator says. How else to explain why two to three hundred people would show up at the Maude Kerns Art Center in Eugene, Oregon, on or about April Fool's Day every year to look at about thirty pieces of Jell-O art?

Ironically, the Jell-O Art Show fund-raiser actually began as a spoof of mainstream art galleries like Maude Kerns by the Radar Angels, an all-gal group of guerrilla

artists locally famous for drawing chalk angels to watch over Eugene buildings and "kidnapping" a favorite science-fiction writer so they could give him a parade.

Their first Jell-O art show in 1983 was not announced in any newspaper or press release but by little posters that directed people to "the warehouse with the purple door." Those who arrived found a hallway of Jell-O art presided over by Angels playing the parts of museum docents and guards.

After three years and growing crowds, the Angels made the show a fund-raiser for Maude Kerns in exchange for help with the sticky postshow cleanup and added a performance based on the new annual themes. In 1998, it was old-time radio and Radar Angel Indra Stern promised the local newspaper reporter who was previewing "Jell-O Air Waves" "a series of vignettes and old songs interspersed with ridiculous verbiage, [that will] make absolutely no sense whatsoever."

Ruth Ann Howden's Jell-O lampshade

There are those who also might question the amount of time some of the Angels have spent creating their Jell-O entries. The most elaborate

Celeste LeBlanc's Jell-O dress

creations have included Shawn Fontain's glittery Jell-O masks, Ruth Ann Howden's Jell-O lampshade, and Celeste LeBlanc's Jell-O dress and jacket. The jacket was made by smearing thick Jell-O over vinyl-backed netting and was later sold by a real art dealer (thereby placing LeBlanc among the world's few professional Jell-O artists).

After more than fifteen years, landscapes or still lifes created by pouring Jell-O into glass-bottom trays are almost common. So are Barbies and Kens. One 1996 entry, for instance, had Barbie sitting in a bathtub of blue Jell-O with a friendly pink-haired troll doll and, in case his intentions weren't already clear, a condom. Eugene being a political town, there are often entries such as the fish-embedded Jell-O brain mold named after a local politician (who fortunately did not attend). There are also conceptual pieces like the lemon Jell-O box placed on top of a one-foot by one-foot yellow Jell-O block entitled "Which Came First?" and the place setting of Jell-O foods next to a thrown napkin and spilled glass labeled, "Jell-Osy."

Representational art has been represented by a Jell-O Greek village, a Jell-O violin, and pizza and beer made out of Jell-O placed in front of a continuously running video loop of football action, naturally.

To keep people from eating the artwork, there is the Tacky Food Buffet of "disgusting but legally edible" foods such as **Jell-O sushi,** deviled Jell-O eggs, and green gelatin sardine cupcakes (which were not a big hit).

It's the one time each year kids from these nutritionally correct northwestern families get to break out and they "love it," Zimmerman said. They loved the life-size naked torso that showed up on the exhibit floor in 1999 (in red) and 2000 (in berry blue) even more. Said Zimmerman, "Kids liked jumping up and down in front of it and seeing the buttocks jiggle."

Should You Find Yourself in Eugene:

There is precedent for considering Jell-O a serious art medium. In the art world, paint made by dissolving pigment in glue or gelatin is known as distemper. Sculptors use plain gelatin as a molding medium, and at least one folk artist paints with a mixture of water, sugar, and colored clay he's dubbed sweet mud.

Anyone can paint and sculpt with Jell-O if you follow the following recipes and advice gleamed from elementary school art teachers, veterans of the annual Jell-O Art Show at the Maude Kerns Art Center in Eugene, Oregon, and the people behind the annual Jell-O sculpture display at the D&R Depot Restaurant in LeRoy, New York.

Paint: Mix Jell-O with water to the consistency of watercolor or acrylic, depending on the desired effect. Jell-O paintings on paper will sparkle when dry. Jell-O clothes can be created by painting high-strength Jell-O on fine-wire mesh. Painting Jell-O on glass looks like stained glass and will last almost as long if allowed to dry.

Tips on Making Nonedible **JELL-O** Art

Finger Paint: Mix Jell-O with hot water, 1 tablespoon at a time until it has a pasty quality. (It will be grainy.) Other art teachers use 2 cups of flour, 1 box Sugar Free Jell-O, and 1/2 cup of salt mixed with 3 cups of boiling water and 3 tablespoons oil.

Play Dough: Mix 1 cup flour, 1/2 cup salt, 1 cup water, 1 tablespoon oil, 2 teaspoons cream of tartar, and 1 small box Sugar Free Jell-O together in a saucepan and cook over medium heat, stirring constantly until it reaches the consistency of mashed potatoes. Cool, then knead with floured hands until dry. Store in airtight container.

Sand Art: Layer different flavors of Jell-O in a jar. Draw things on paper with glue, then sprinkle Jell-O on the glue (lightly blowing away any excess). Make an edible rock garden by spreading a half-inch layer of Jell-O in a cake pan and adding candy rocks.

Dioramas: The debut of berry blue Jell-O revitalized the diorama as a school project. Jell-O aquariums with Pepperidge Farm goldfish or Swedish fish (inserted with a toothpick when the Jell-O is partly set) and parsley, in particular, have become almost too common to create any excitement. (You need to add a plastic shark and diver and a bit of grenadine blood for that.) Or try a beach scene using berry blue Jell-O water, crushed cookie sand, and drink parasols as beach umbrellas. For a farm or forest scene, make dirt-colored Jell-O by mixing lemon and grape, or lime and any red flavor. For the night sky or the aftermath of a forest fire mix orange and grape.

Sculpture: Most people start with the Jigglers recipe (1/2 cup boiling water for every 3-ounce box of Jell-O). Using less water and/or adding Knox unflavored gelatin will give a sculpture added strength. So will letting it dehydrate in the open air for several days. Generally speaking contained sculpture and small pieces don't need to be as firm as freestanding and bigger pieces. Some people will try to save money by just using unflavored gelatin and food coloring but that doesn't taste very good and is more apt to crack than Jell-O, whose sugar adds elasticity and body.

The Experiment

Finally, an explanation for the popularity of Yanni, nose rings, and superstrong breath mints: People have Jell-O for brains.

Dr. Adrian R. M. Upton proved it by hooking up an electroencephalograph (EEG) machine to a mound of lime Jell-O and comparing the readouts to the same test done on healthy human beings. They were almost identical.

Dr. Upton first did this in Britain in 1969, and got the same result when he repeated the test in the intensive care unit of McMaster University Medical Centre in Hamilton, Ontario, in 1974.

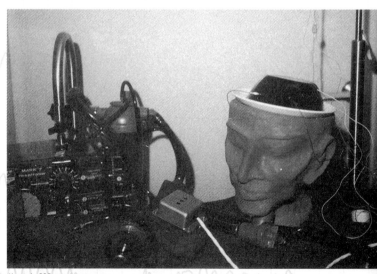

Upton's EEG test in progress

The question is, why did he do it? Was he trying to explain the stupidity of a particular set of medical students? Secure grant money from Jell-O owner General Foods?

Actually, Upton says, it was to show that stray electrical signals given off by respirators, intravenous feeders, and human movement in a hospital ward produce readings on patient EEGs that could fool doctors into thinking a person's brain is still living when, in fact, it might be as lifeless as a bowl of Jell-O.

Upton's experiments proved the flat EEG readout most hospitals then required to declare a patient brain dead was extremely difficult to achieve in a typical hospital setting. The consistency and density of the human brain is quite similar to Jell-O. That's one of the reasons the McMaster University Medical Centre neurology head chose it for his experiments. He chose lime green "because I thought it would be more photogenic," he said.

After reading a report about Upton's Ontario experiment in the April 5, 1976, issue of *Hospital Tribune*, one Florida physician wrote of his worries that with its "beautiful brain waves . . . it is possible that the Jell-O may be accepted into law school, might end up holding higher office, and become engaged in making rules and regulations for the conduct of medicine." Another physician asked Upton to fly to New York to consult on a critical blancmange case. A report on the experiment even made the Australian edition of *Playboy* (the text part, Upton emphasizes), and news of it still floats around on the Internet, though rarely in connection with its serious aim.

Thank goodness Upton has a sense of humor. He also has the satisfaction of knowing that, thanks to his Jell-O studies "physicians and technicians now take interference into account when taking EEGs."

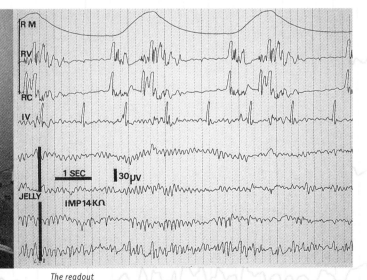

The readout

The Building

For years it was the first stop on one local tourism operator's "Seven Wonders of Seattle" tour. And it's no wonder. It's not every day that you get to see a building festooned with four hundred Jell-O molds. "When the light breaks, it's like a million suns!" said Hector Izquierdo of the building in April 1997.

But four months later this shining light of Seattle kitsch culture was extinguished permanently to make way for a high-rise, and the Jell-O Mold Building joined the Dog House restaurant and perpetually rising Microsoft stock as part of city myth and memory.

The building was hardly any shining sun when a group of artists known as SCUD (Subterranean Co-operative of Urban Dreams) first moved into 2400 Western Avenue in the mid-1980s. Then, it was just an abandoned building in the city's gritty Belltown neighborhood whose across-street neighbor was a soup kitchen–cum–day labor agency ironically named the Millionair Club. The twelve artists spent six months hauling off garbage and making repairs before they could even move in. Once they did, they ate, made art, and partied as one. "Every time anyone . . . threw a party, we got just one invitation marked 'To SCUD,'" recalled former member Ashleigh Talbot.

A club, Free Mars, that one member opened in the basement also made the building a mecca for other artists and musicians, including the Grateful Dead. The successor coffeehouse, Cyclops, was a favorite with writers like William Burroughs, cartoonist R. Crumb, and rockers Iggy Pop, Soundgarden, and Pearl Jam. Nirvana's Kurt Cobain was such good friends with Cyclops owner Gina Kaukola that he gave her one of his gold records. By 1992, Cyclops had become an icon of artistic Seattle, one

Diane Szukovathy carrying mold and art supplies

that director Cameron Crowe captured in promotional bits for an ABC concert music show.

The building only got cooler after being painted bright purple and lime green. (Those colors were chosen via a random throwing of a book of paint swatches down one of the building's hallways.) Artist Diane Szukovathy added the Jell-O molds as a way to make the storefront trim live up to the color scheme.

She got most from thrift shops but also bolted a donation box to the side of the building that yielded forty more, many of which came with long Jell-O family histories.

Once mounted, these metal circles, stars, cones, cornucopias, flying fish, eagles, Kewpie dolls, and Scooby-Doos made the building "look like one of those elaborate packages of multicolored candy," Szukovathy said. In other words, it was beautiful—way too beautiful, in fact, to stay a low-rent artists' building in a part of the city that was becoming increasingly gentrified.

In 1996, the building's owners announced plans to build a new high-rise on the Jell-O Mold Building site. Almost immediately, two separate groups took up the Jell-O building cause. The Campaign for Belltown Preservation and Culture collected almost twenty-four hundred signatures to no avail.

Though the Jell-O Mold Building was destroyed, the molds were saved. Some now decorate hose bibs and pathways in a community garden in Mount Baker, a "regular folks" section of Seattle, according to Szukovathy, who sincerely hopes it will stay that way.

The Jell-O Mold Building in Seattle

The Restaurant

The 1960s ad slogan says there's always room for Jell-O. But at Charles Shamoon's Raleigh, North Carolina, mall restaurant called Jiggles, there's *only* room for Jell-O. The store sells almost nothing but Jell-O gelatin and pudding desserts and some drinks to wash them down with.

Shamoon says the idea of creating the country's first (and still) only Jell-Ocatessen came to him while praying for a good idea for a business. (Apparently even Our Heavenly Father loves Jell-O.) Growing up working in his earthly father's grocery store, Shamoon had also noticed that Jell-O was one of the only very popular supermarket foods that did not yet have its own restaurant venue.

Armed with both divine inspiration and this insider information, Shamoon opened his first all-Jell-O restaurant in 1991 in his native Greenville, Mississippi, in a freestanding building.

"That was mistake number one," says the gentlemanly Shamoon in his heavy Southern accent. "This is a product that lends itself to impulse purchase, something that happens much more when people are walking rather than when they're driving."

Mistake number two was in calling the place "Hello . . . I'm Jell-O" without first calling trademark attorneys at Kraft General Foods. So they called him—once a day for nine months until he agreed to change it to the generic, "Hello . . . I'm Gellatin" (and later, Hello . . . I'm Jiggles, or just Jiggles).

Shamoon moved the store from Greenville to mall locations in Augusta and suburban Atlanta, Georgia, before settling more or less permanently in the food court of

Raleigh's Crabtree Valley Mall where its revenues rival nearby ice-cream and cookie stands.

Here as elsewhere the biggest challenge is "the misconception people have about the kind of Jell-O we're serving. They think the plain kind in cubes or with the rubbery tops." Shamoon says there's been no excuse for rubbery tops since the invention of Saran Wrap, and that his Jell-O desserts are anything but plain. They include elaborate Jell-O gelatin parfaits and Jell-O pudding whips that glisten under display case floodlights like a little indoor aurora borealis.

"My cases are breathtaking," he confirms in what sounds like a boast but is really a necessity in a business where "you have a maximum of about ten seconds to make a sale."

The Raleigh restaurant best-sellers include Jolly Pops, a Turkish taffylike treat he molds in Dixie Cups, slices into disks, and sticks on straws; a parfait made with mandarin oranges, sherbet, pineapple, and vanilla pudding, and an Oreo-studded blend of Jell-O chocolate pudding and Cool Whip. His four hundred-recipe repertoire also includes Jell-O shrimp salad, Jell-O popcorn, and Jell-O pizza (a sweet kind consisting of a cookie crust, strawberry Jell-O sauce, and sliced strawberries and bananas).

Shamoon got his recipes from Kraft, his late mother, his own imagination, and customers who are forever handing him hand-printed recipe cards featuring their favorites.

"Everyone loves Jell-O," Shamoon says. By association, "I feel like the whole United States is embracing me with love and compassion."

Jolly Pops

Here's how to make Jell-O lollipops like those sold at Raleigh, North Carolina, Jiggles's gelatin kiosk.

1 1/4 cups boiling water
2 (3-ounce) packages or 1 (6-ounce) package Jell-O gelatin, any flavor

Stir boiling water into gelatin. Dissolve completely. Allow to cool for 15 minutes. Pour into 5-ounce Dixie paper cups. Refrigerate at least 3 hours. Carefully peel off paper cups. Cut each gelatin cup horizontally into 3 round slices. Push a straw into each gelatin circle to create a lollipop. Makes 12 pops.

The Space Flight

Astronaut Shannon Lucid joined the crew of the late Russian space station, Mir, in March 1996 to do research involving protein crystals, quail eggs, deforestation, and the effects of long-term weightlessness on the human body.

When she returned to earth that September, it was as the most experienced NASA astronaut of either sex, with more time in space than any American and any woman from any country.

To her Russian cosmonaut colleagues, however, Lucid is probably best known for her Jell-O.

Unlike the NASA space shuttles, Mir was outfitted with a refrigerator. Lucid had also been told that the Russians loved gelatin. So before she left on her six-month experiment in outer space international relations, she asked the NASA food lab if they could put some Jell-O powder in the foil containers normally used for drinks. As when making drinks, Lucid added water with a syringe, then refrigerated the bag. When it had jelled, she cut the top off and she and her two space colleagues ate it with spoons. "Jell-O is pretty sticky so if you're careful it won't fly away," she said.

Shannon Lucid and Yuri Usachev enjoying their Sunday treat on Mir

Lucid served the Jell-O for the first time on Easter Sunday and then every Sunday night thereafter. Her Russian crewmates loved the stuff so much they kept asking, "Isn't today Sunday?" like impatient children on a long trip. To which she would reply, "No, it's not. No Jell-O tonight!" In the rapidly orbiting space station, "where light follows darkness every 45 minutes, it is important . . . to have simple ways of marking the passage of time," Lucid wrote in one e-mail back to earth. Her Sunday rituals of eating Jell-O and wearing pink socks helped her do that.

The Jell-O was also a good bribe when Lucid needed help finding an athletic shoe she lost on the messy Mir. Usually the three crew members would share one Jell-O drink package but as a prize for finding Lucid's shoe, flight engineer Yuri Usachev got to eat a whole one all by himself.

In fact, Lucid went so far as to call gelatin "the greatest improvement in space flight since my first flight over 10 years ago."

And when it was time for Lucid to go, Mir commander Valery Korzun offered this tribute: "The most delicious desserts are here thanks to Shannon, and now that Shannon is going back to earth she has left these delicacies to us."

The JELL-O Hoax

Paul Heckbert is not the only person to have written a joke scientific paper about Jell-O. In fact, the comic *Journal of Irreproducible Results* published a whole issue of such papers in 1992.

But Heckbert has got to be one of the only scientists to deliver his Jell-O paper at a serious academic conference, and to actually initiate a storm of criticism against that appearance from among his professional colleagues.

It all started, as many silly things do, with a few beers Heckbert was tossing back with some computer graphics colleagues from Pixar animation studios. Talk turned to the ridiculous esotericism of papers in their subspecialty of ray tracing, which involves using mathematical formulas to generate realistic-looking pictures on a computer. Heckbert tried to think of the most ridiculous thing somebody could ray trace. Jell-O came to mind. But

instead of doing what most people in his semi-inebriated state would do—enjoy a good chuckle and forget about it—Heckbert submitted the idea to one of the most prestigious conferences in his field.

To his surprise, his paper was accepted, complete with tongue-in-cheek reviewers' comments, and Heckbert was invited to present it at the 1987 Special Interest Group on Graphics (SIGGRAPH) conference. The paper, "Ray Tracing Jell-O Brand Gelatin," was later published in two computer graphics journals and *Seminal Graphics*, a book compilation of significant early computer graphics research.

While the paper contains a fair number of computer graphics in-jokes, anyone who has written a college term paper should be able to relate to this sentence from a section about Jell-O's wiggliness entitled "Jell-O Dynamics." "From previous research with rendering systems, we have learned that a good dose of gratuitous partial differential equations is needed to meet the paper quota for impressive formulas," Heckbert concludes, before giving a bunch.

Later, in the "Implementation" section, Heckbert admits, "To create a picture using the full Jell-O Engine simulation, we estimate that 1 CPU eon of CRAY time and a lot of hard work would be required. We made several simplifying approximations, however, since the article is due today."

The Soupy Sales Show is listed among the article's citations. The figure 7 illustration, "Preliminary results from the Jell-O Engine," looks suspiciously like a photograph of a Jell-O mold on a bathroom tile floor.

Heckbert only got about seven minutes to present his paper at SIGGRAPH. He said most people seemed amused, although a few wondered aloud whether his talk might have prevented a serious paper from being presented. At least one attendee thought it *was* a serious paper judging from the earnest questions he asked Heckbert following the talk.

That would have been satisfaction enough for most jokesters but not Heckbert, who saw the subsequent posting of his paper on a computer graphics Internet discussion board as an opportunity to extend the joke even further. So he answered the posting with the following flame: "Please get this garbage off the net! We're carrying on a serious technical discussion here and we don't need this sort of facetious drivel tying up the phone lines and wasting my tax dollars!"

A debate about Heckbert's Jell-O paper raged for two days until somebody noticed his e-mail address in the original message. One critical posting entitled "The joke's on Paul" predicted, "Long after everyone's forgotten all of Paul's serious professional papers, 'Ray Tracing Jell-O Brand Gelatin' will live on."

Now an associate professor at Carnegie Mellon, Heckbert himself admits that it is "the most widely read paper I've ever written."

The Web Site

The most comprehensive independent Jell-O site on the World Wide Web was inspired by a column in *Playboy* magazine. Computer programmer Chaz Boston Baden says he actually *reads Playboy* and once you get a look at the nerdy picture of him on his home page (he's wearing teddy bear ears), it's easy to believe.

The topic in the Playboy Advisor column was Jell-O shots (drinks made by substituting alcohol for the cold water in the standard Jell-O recipe). It ended by suggesting that readers have fun experimenting with different flavors of Jell-O and types of liquor. Baden decided to do just that, and started toting the results to parties.

By the early 1990s, Baden's identity was so wrapped up in the recipe he had developed for margarita Jell-O shots that the standard signature line on all his e-mail messages included information on how to get a copy. The requests came pouring in with many questions and other Jell-O recipes so Baden eventually decided to post them all on a computer bulletin board he dubbed the Jellophile.

The primitive graphics of the 'phile's current Web incarnation hint of these early Internet origins. In fact, its most visually interesting element is the smiley face Baden has put in the *O* of Jell-O. Contentwise, however, the seven-chapter Jellophile rivals Kraft's official Jell-O Web site in authoritativeness and is even more complete

Recipes from the 'Phile

Here are two recipes from the Jellophile Web site's extensive collection. The first is a virgin variation of the margarita Jell-O recipe that started it all; the second is a recipe for a spider cake that spews its gelatin guts—a sure hit with the kids.

Virgin Strawberry Margarita

1 (3-ounce) package strawberry Jell-O gelatin
1 cup boiling water
1/4 cup fresh lime juice
3/4 cup cold water

Dissolve the Jell-O in boiling water. Add lime juice and cold water. Pour into an ice cube tray, a pan, or Dixie cups, and chill until firm.

Spider Cake

1 (18.5-ounce) box cake mix
1 (3-ounce) package lime Jell-O gelatin
1 (16-ounce) can prepared chocolate frosting
Blue food coloring
4 black licorice sticks
Green gumdrops or gum balls, 2 large and 6 small

Prepare cake mix according to package directions, then pour into 2 well-greased metal mixing bowls (one bigger than the other). Bake, unmold, and set aside.

Prepare Jell-O according to package directions, then chill until very thick. Beat with electric beater until Jell-O has about doubled its volume.

Slice the bigger cake in half horizontally. Carefully scoop out a cavity in each half. Fill the cavities with the Jell-O, then reattach the halves and top with smaller cake. Place on a large serving platter.

Mix one or two drops of blue food coloring into the frosting to make it turn black. Frost entire spider body. Use licorice sticks for legs and gumdrops as eyes. When cut into, the cake will spurt green goop to simulate a real spider. Serves 16.

because it includes the alcoholic recipes that Kraft shuns (at www.boston baden.com/hazel/Jello/jello.html).

Baden's alcoholic Jell-O "desserts" still make up the bulk of the Jellophile. Baden calls them alcoholic desserts rather than shots because of their relatively modest alcohol content (Baden's shots have a 75/25 ratio of water to alcohol instead of the traditional 50/50). But he also offers virgin variations, a section of offbeat nonshot Jell-O recipes, and a strong technical section that tells how to substitute Knox for Jell-O in a recipe (and vice versa), how to make Jell-O firmer, and the best way to make Jell-O glow (this requires a flashlight rather than radioactive materials).

The Web's worldwide reach also makes this the best place to find out how gelatin is eaten elsewhere. Baden backs up international visitors' comments with a "picture gallery" of gelatin boxes from Canada, Mexico, and elsewhere.

But the Jellophile's alcoholic origins show in the section devoted to Jell-O Tips and Tricks, which, in addition to instructions about unmolding and adding fruit that you'd find in any official Jell-O cookbook, includes an extensive discussion of the best containers for Jell-O shots: three-ounce Dixie cups, two-ounce clear plastic salsa cups, or one-ounce disposable shot glasses. The one-ouncers are usually popped into the mouth—container and all—and are highly recommended by one frat boy Jellophile contributor for the fun of watching people's faces contort as they try to dislodge the Jell-O with their tongues.

Where Was William?

In 1998, Kraft erected a Jell-O billboard in New York's Times Square and launched a "How Jell-O makes you smile" contest for essays to be featured on the billboard.

Catherine Weber's poem won because it showed the part the packaged food played in her loving relationship with her son William, explained a Jell-O executive.

So it's perhaps not surprising that the first words out of Kraft employees who met the Weber family during the New York City trip they won was, Where's William?

The answer: at home in suburban Detroit because the trip was only for a family of four, the Webers are a family of six, and his mother thought three-and-a-half-year-old William too young to drag around New York City.

And so, while two of William's sisters went to Broadway shows, met Bill Cosby, and watched a poem about their brother light up Times Square, William was pulling a Macaulay Culkin with his Jell-O rainbow.

OK, So She's Not Dana Gioia

Here's Catherine Weber's award winner.

At three-and-a-half William said to me
"Mommy, when I grow up a rainbow I will be."
"Let's build a rainbow," I said in reply
Remembering the Jell-O boxes nearby
Sweet cherry . . . lemon so bright . . .
Fresh lime . . . cool berry blue—just right.
We spoke of love, friendship and laughter,
Words about life and peace followed after.
Simple. Like Jell-O, the lessons begin.
The rainbow he found came from within.
He smiled.
I smiled.

The happy Weber family (sans William) in front of the Jell-O billboard

The **JELL-O** Billboard: By the Numbers

Date unveiled: May 19, 1998

Billboard dimensions: 55 by 105 feet

Number of spoons displayed thereon: 3,850

Number of three-ounce packages of Jell-O needed to feed 3,850 spoon bearers: 963

Size of the largest spoon: 52 feet

Size of neon Jell-O logo: 14 by 52 feet

Approximate cost of billboard's three-year lease: $4 million

Average number of people who visit Times Square each day: 1.7 million

Cost of each potential individual billboard viewing: $1/5$ of a cent

Number of entries in the essay contest for Jell-O memories to be featured on the billboard's electronic display: 6,000

Percentage importance of "clarity of thought" in judging criteria for the essay contest: 25

Maximum number of words allowed in essay: 75

Number of words in winning essay: 75

Approximate retail value of the essay contest grand prize of a four-day/three-night trip for four to New York for the billboard unveiling: $6,400

Amount New York's Parks Commission said they would fine event planners working on the Jell-O billboard unveiling if they damaged the dogwood trees while putting up their stage, per tree: $30,000

Date dismantled: April 19, 2000

Chapter 8

STARRING JELL-O

*E*veryone knows that Jell-O gelatin offers a world of possibility for tasty salads and desserts, and it's not surprising that colorful and shiny Jell-O would inspire painting and sculpture.

But did you know that this highly malleable substance has also been used to create film special effects, beautiful music, and serious social commentary?

The many Jell-O appearances in movies, TV shows, theater, novels, poetry, and artwork could be read as a sign of Jell-O's importance in our culture. Or not.

Animal Antics The most famous Jell-O scene on stage or screen by far occurs in the Faber College cafeteria in the 1978 movie *National Lampoon's Animal House.* Slovenly Delta fraternity brother Bluto Blutarsky (played by John Belushi) walks down the cafeteria line picking up everything in sight. He loads down his tray, stuffs his pockets, and after a quick glance around to make sure no one's watching, noisily inhales a square of green Jell-O on the spot.

Bluto sits down at a table with members of the rival Omega House fraternity and begins to wolf down the food in a manner Amy Vanderbilt could never have imagined even in her worst nightmares. Seeing the prissy Omegas and their girlfriends' looks of disgust, Bluto grabs another square of lime Jell-O and sucks as much as he can into his mouth at once.

"That boy is a P-I-G," says one of the girls in a strong southern accent.

"See if you can guess what I am now," replies Bluto, as he stuffs his cheeks with mashed potatoes, then smacks them with his hands, spewing potatoes. "I'm a zit!" he screams as the Omegas begin chase and the famous food fight begins.

The whole scene only takes three minutes of screen time. But a new word entered the American vernacular to describe the way Belushi ate his first square of Jell-O: snarfing. It refers to the art of consuming foods without either chewing or swallowing. Shortly after *Animal House* was released, Jell-O snarfing contests and toga parties became a fixture of college spring break fun.

John Belushi's widow, Judy Belushi Pisano, says snarfing had its origins in an after-hours restaurant cleanup job Belushi had when he was in college. Before Belushi and the other two guys on the cleanup crew would begin work, they would chow down. "There was this big refrigerator filled with trays and trays of Jell-O. That's where he discovered that Jell-O could be pulled up like that," Pisano says.

And that's why when it came time to film the cafeteria scene in *Animal House*, Belushi told the show's producers to "make sure there was some Jell-O in there."

Divine Dessert

Jell-O is also credited with one on-screen miracle. It was in Cecil B. DeMille's 1923 silent film *The Ten Commandments.*

The most spectacular moment in this film version of the Exodus story is when Moses parts the Red Sea. How to do that without divine intervention was the problem DeMille assigned to Paramount special effects whiz Roy Pomeroy.

Pomeroy solved it by shooting some footage of two huge dump tanks depositing water into a U-shaped trough. Run in reverse, this looked more or less like a body of water being divided. The tougher part was keeping the two walls of water apart so the Israelites could walk through. Pomeroy reportedly got his idea by watching a child play with some pudding. He used gelatin because it was firmer and so could part the water more definitively.

To be specific, Pomeroy cut a slice out of the center of a large gelatin mold, took pictures of some fleeing actors, then superimposed the actors onto the center of his mold footage (at least that's how Pomeroy's assistant, T. K. Peters, said he did it; DeMille refused to talk about such trade secrets).

Pomeroy also parted the Red Sea in DeMille's 1956 remake of *The Ten Commandments* by playing a film of some ocean tides in reverse. No Jell-O was involved.

Wizard Dust

The American food classic of many colors and the American film classic *The Wizard of Oz* came together in the scene featuring a horse of many colors.

Dorothy is initially rebuffed by the gateman to Emerald City but when she shows him her ruby slippers, he exclaims, "That's a horse of a different color!" A few moments later Dorothy and company enter Emerald City in a carriage drawn by just such a horse or, actually, several different horses.

Given how many times and how quickly the horse was supposed to change color, using one horse was impractical. So six white horses were enlisted. The original idea of painting the horses was nixed by the Society for the Prevention of Cruelty to Animals. Food coloring was tried but the colors were too bright. Finally somebody got the bright idea of sponging the horses down with Jell-O powder. Six handlers were needed to keep the horses from snacking between takes.

Disaster Dessert

Jell-O made high-flying appearances in the 1980 airplane disaster movie spoof *Airplane!* and its 1982 sequel.

In *Airplane!* a doctor predicts that some tainted fish will soon reduce the pilot "to a quivering, wasted piece of jelly," just seconds before the pilot drops to the floor and the plane starts lurching. The camera makes a quick cut to a shot of a seat tray table bearing a violently quivering Jell-O mold, then pans to a shot of a female passenger's similarly bouncing breasts.

In a similar moment of crisis in *Airplane II: The Sequel*, Julie Hagerty begs for help from a passenger with flight experience by telling him that the pilot has been gassed and the copilot has "turned to jelly," as the camera cuts to a cockpit shot of a copilot's uniform topped by a red gelatin head.

Marge's Molds

Marge Simpson's love of Jell-O is the stuff of legend.

That could be because her skill at making gelatin molds was established in a first-year episode in which she prepared a whole counterful of them for husband Homer's company picnic.

"Are you sure that's enough?" Homer asks after surveying the spread. "You know how the boss loves your delicious gelatin desserts!" When Marge points out that his boss only said he liked them once, Homer replies, Yeah, but it was "the only time he's ever spoken to me without using the word Bonehead."

Marge turns out to be right. Because when they get to the picnic and present their gelatin offerings to boss Burns, he snaps, "Oh, for the love of Peter! Some damn fool went around telling everyone I love that slimy goop. Toss it in the pile over there," as the camera pans to a room full of undulating molds.

And that's only the beginning of many gelatin references made on the series. In a 1994 episode where the Simpsons find relief from a heat wave by lounging in their open refrigerator, little Maggie falls asleep on a Jell-O mold. At a 1997 outdoor party, Homer comments on Marge's love of Jell-O shooters.

Bart Simpson also likes Jell-O. In fact, the food chapter of the book *Bart Simpson's Guide to Life* begins with a picture of Bart peering through a gelatin mold. Gelatin is also the focus of one of four food groups recommended by the Bart Simpson Nutritional Institute in that same book—that group being Wiggly. (The other three are Sticky, Runny, and Puffy.)

The Simpsons are only the latest in a long line of blue-collar TV families with Jell-O ties. (The Bunkers of *All in the Family* and the Conners of *Roseanne* also ate it.) It only makes sense, considering Jell-O's popularity in families with multiple kids.

At least one former Jell-O executive thinks there is more to the Simpsons' obsession with Jell-O than simple demographics. Former General Foods dessert marketing chief Dana Gioia thinks the multiple gelatin mentions are part revenge over a Jell-O–Simpsons advertising deal that never quite jelled.

A story in a September 1999 issue of *Adweek* reported that Simpsons creator Matt Groening and executives from Jell-O ad agency Young & Rubicam were talking about the possibility of having Bart warble the old J-E-L-L-O jingle in an ad when Groening suddenly had a brainstorm. "Wouldn't it be funny if Bart belched on the *O*?"

The ad folks didn't think so. And that's why Bart now warns people not to "lay a finger on my Butterfinger" instead of the Jell-O his family loves even more.

Late Night with Gelatin

Jell-O sightings on late-night talk shows date back to the '50s, when original *Tonight Show* host Steve Allen

dove into nine feet of it. David Letterman did back-to-back Jell-O stunts one week in 1988—throwing a Jell-O mold off a five-story building one night, then showing a slow-motion replay of pool balls falling into a Jell-O tub the next.

It's also been featured in a number of his Top 10 lists, including 1992's "Top 10 Rejected Plots for the Final Episode of 'The Cosby Show'" (Rudy gets in trouble when she tells her father, "Jell-O sucks!"), 1998's "Cool Things about Winning a Gold Medal" (Get to do Jell-O shots with Dave's mom), and 1999's "Least Important Inventions of the 20th Century" (Osmond-flavored Jell-O).

Where All the Salads Are Made of JELL-O

Being set in a small town in Minnesota filled with churchgoing Lutherans, Garrison Keillor's *A Prairie Home Companion* is filled with Jell-O references. It cropped up in a song about what it means to be a Lutheran, a joke show riddle about Iowans' denseness (Why don't Iowans make Jell-O? They can't figure how out how to get two cups of water in those little bags.), and in a Guy Noir detective skit where Jell-O on a restaurant menu helps a new Minnesota resident understand that she's not in New York City anymore.

Jell-O was also the subject of one of sound effect man Tom Keith's greatest challenges: creating the noise a pig would make jumping into a tub of the stuff.

But the most memorable reference to Jell-O on the public radio show occurred in Keillor's 1985 monologue "Bruno, the Fishing Dog." It is the story of upwardly mobile Minneapolis resident Bob Johnson, his aging mother Lena, and his equally aging dog Bruno.

As the story begins, Bruno is wrapping up his usual two-month summer vacation with Lena in small-town Lake Wobegon, most of which he spends down at the lake trying and failing to re-create youthful fishing triumphs. Bob and his wife, Merlette, have recently had a new baby.

Arriving at their home for the reception just after the baptism with Bruno and a dessert made with cherry Jell-O, mandarin oranges, and miniature marshmallows, Lena finds the Johnson home filled with strangers, including caterers who quickly whisk her dessert into the refrigerator. Given the fancy spread the caterers had laid out, "Lena knew she was not going to see that Jell-O again."

And then Bruno appears, his eyes lock on the smoked trout that is the centerpiece of the buffet, and his fishing instincts take over. In an instant he's out the door with the smoked trout in his mouth leaving a maelstrom of broken dishes, fresh-cut vegetables, and "little things on sticks."

Lena works quickly to clean everything up and a few moments later, returns triumphant with her Jell-O dish, asking, "Would anyone care for dessert?"

Blue Men and Orange JELL-O

Food plays an important role in the Marshall McLuhan—meets—*Animal House* madness that is *Blue Man Group: Tubes.* In the course of the ninety-minute theatrical happening three silent, bald, blue-colored men create an abstract sculpture out of regurgitated marshmallows and a symphony out of eating Cap'n Crunch. Moments after they eat Twinkies, its gooey cream filling spurts out of their chests.

Jell-O gets two scenes in the long-running show.

First, one of the Blue Men tries to woo a female audience member with a feast of Jell-O and Twinkies. When wobbling the tiny orange Jell-O mold fails to impress, he launches it into the audience. Then he picks up a Twinkie and tries to wobble it too.

The Men take another audience member backstage and turn him into a giant human paintbrush by slathering his clothes with paint, tying his feet to a rope, and swinging his body against a giant white

Blue Man Group and gelatin mold.

canvas. A few moments later the mad blue magicians wheel a huge orange Jell-O mold onstage—which suddenly erupts to reveal the head of the hapless victim.

To accomplish these stunts in the four productions of *Tubes* now playing around the country requires thirty gallons of Jell-O per performance (which is like tiny Jell-O shots compared to the tons of toilet paper used to trash the theaters). The giant Jell-O is molded into a planter; the small one, in a restaurant takeout container. In New York they're both made by Glorious Foods, the tony catering company where Blue Men Chris Wink and Phil Stanton met while working parties for the likes of Jackie Onassis and Brooke Astor. Glorious Foods' Chef Jean-Claude Nedelac is even credited in the *Tubes* playbill as "Jello [*sic*] consultant."

Wink and Stanton's waiter experience is not the reason there's so much food in *Tubes*. Food is such an important part of the pop cultural landscape that *Tubes* means to comment about. Wink says they used Jell-O because it's "the ultimate twentieth-century pop cultural foodstuff." It's both "a sign of the decline of western civilization" but also "fun, exuberant, and an embodiment of the life force."

Like Trying to Juggle JELL-O

One of the most popular pieces in the Flying Karamazov Brothers' repertoire of comic juggling acts is one in which Ivan (Howard Patterson) juggles three items brought in by the audience members. One of the most popular items audiences bring is Jell-O.

Patterson says he's probably juggled Jell-O "several hundred times, both with and without fruit fillings" since the group started doing this part of the show, called the Gamble or the Challenge.

How hard is juggling Jell-O?

Patterson says that depends on how hot it is onstage, how the Jell-O was prepared, and what else you have to juggle with it. (If the other items include a condom full of baked beans, a paint bucket, a trombone, a nine-foot octopus, a Slinky, a chocolate cream pie, or a plastic bag containing 150 dead frogs in formaldehyde—to name a few Patterson has actually juggled for the Gamble—it's obviously going to be pretty difficult.)

In the early days, people were nice enough to bring Jell-O Jigglers, which are fairly firm, making them easy to juggle. Later conventional recipe Jell-O became all the rage and it "tended to fragment in the air into smaller and smaller and wetter and wetter pieces until I was basically juggling little red water droplets [i.e., nothing]," Patterson says.

In fact, Patterson has been known to keep hot water and a towel backstage so he wouldn't have to do the rest of the show sticky from Jell-O.

Jello the Man

How did one of punk rock's great provocateurs end up with the same name as one of mainstream America's favorite desserts?

Dead Kennedys lead singer Jello Biafra was born Eric Boucher and called himself Occupant after he first moved to San Francisco in the late 1970s. He chose the name because that was how most of his mail was addressed. It was only when he got into the punk scene, and people started confusing him with the cult band Residents that he changed it to Jello (the happy all-American food) and Biafra (then a worldwide symbol of third-world starvation) because "I liked the way the two images collide in the mind."

Jello Biafra

Jello the man has had only fleeting run-ins with Jell-O the food. Biafra supporters borrowed the food's famous "There's always room for Jell-O" slogan for Biafra's unsuccessful 1979 campaign to be mayor of San Francisco, although Biafra says it was no more his official slogan than "What if he wins?" (That slogan presumably the work of someone who had heard of his proposal to create an official city Board of Bribery and require all downtown businessmen to dress in clown suits.) Biafra didn't win but he did come in fourth, with 4 percent of the vote.

Biafra says people often ask him "what flavor I am, as though they're really witty and they're the first person to ever think of this." He said that people would sometimes throw boxes of Jell-O at the stage during Dead Kennedys concerts. "If they were open, there would be this sugar dust flying through the air, which was not real good for the respiratory system."

Biafra has also never much cared for conventionally prepared gelatin although he doesn't have anything against other people eating it. Although many of his songs and speeches warn against the dangers of corporate feudalism in America, he's never recommended a Jell-O boycott.

"I think there are a lot more important things to boycott." In fact, he says, "I suspect Jell-O is actually a lot safer than genetically engineered corn and soybeans and other Frankenfood."

One Fine Rhyme

Jell-O gets a mention in the show tune–turned–jazz standard, "A Fine Romance." It was written by Jerome Kern and Dorothy Fields for the 1936 movie *Swing Time* and first sung by Ginger Rogers to Fred Astaire. The song is about the lack of romanticism in their romance, although the line about Jell-O—*You take romance, I'll take Jell-O*—is one of the least clear lines in the song.

Was Fields saying that Jell-O is sexy? Or was she just desperate to find something to rhyme with fellow? (We suspect the latter.)

At least people still know what Jell-O *is*—which is more than can be said about the Seidlitz powder the song also mentions.

Green Jellö The Band

Former members of Green Jellö like to boast that they were one of the worst bands in punk rock history.

That's why they called themselves Green Jellö.

"The idea was to name the world's worst band after the most disgusting flavor of the world's worst food," says former member Gary Helsinger, although he admits that most of those at the naming session were "probably high."

Green Jellö was started in 1981 by some Buffalo, New York, high school pals who knew so little about music that they played songs by color coding their guitar frets.

To distract from the incompetence of their playing and the silliness of songs like "Jump" (about people jumping), they dressed as Fred Flintstone and Barney Rubble in punk haircuts, Froot Loops spokesbird Toucan Sam, a cow, a rat, even a piece of manure. Helsinger appeared at one Buffalo concert wearing only a sock (it wasn't on his foot), which came off while he was doing some vigorous dancing.

Similar antics got the group gonged off *The Gong Show* in 1987, which probably would have been the group's career highlight if leader Bill Manspeaker hadn't managed to talk someone at Zoo Entertainment into paying them to make a video. It turned into a surprise hit and spawned an equally successful audio soundtrack. During the concert tour that followed, fans showered them with chunks of green Jell-O.

This publicity and the subsequent fame led the group to be named "Musical Lowpoint of 1993" by *Rolling Stone.* It also brought the group and its outrageous antics to the attention of Jell-O trademark attorneys who asked them in no uncertain terms to change their name to Green Jellÿ. Cease-and-desist letters followed from the companies behind the Flintstones and Toucan Sam, and soon, Green Jellÿ was back to playing local clubs.

This probably has less to do with the group's legal troubles than what Manspeaker himself freely admitted. "We know it's really stupid and the songs are bad. . . . We suck in all honesty."

Song Surprise

It's probably not going out on a limb to say that William Bolcom is the only composer to have written a song about a Jell-O mold and won a Pulitzer (although the prize was for his "New Etudes for Piano" and not the Jell-O song).

He wrote it one day in 1972 when he and his wife, mezzo-soprano Joan Morris, were visiting Portland, Oregon's, famous Henry Thiele's. "Little pouter-pigeon ladies with pillbox hats filled the restaurant, little fingers aloft as they sipped tea," reminding Bolcom of

the countless club ladies he had entertained as a piano prodigy. He pulled out a notebook and began writing down this ode to the outrageous concoctions these ladies made and ate.

It's my Lime Jello [sic], Marshmallow, Cottage Cheese Surprise!
With slices of pimento, you won't believe your eyes! . . .
Truly a creation that description defies . . .
I did not steal that recipe, it's lies, I tell you, lies! . . .

After reading the complete finished lyric, Morris declared it "too silly" to perform. Nevertheless, she did perform it three years later as a wedding present to him. "Lime Jello . . ." was the title tune on the couple's 1986 RCA Red Seal live album and has become a highlight of the American song concerts Bolcom and Morris jointly perform—approximations of this dish now being the chief peril of the postconcert receptions.

Diner Downer

It may not be surprising that the songwriter behind *You're a Good Man, Charlie Brown* and the children's TV show *Captain Kangaroo* would have written a song about Jell-O. What is surprising is the negative tone of the title tune of Clark Gesner's 1998 Off-Broadway revue, *The Jello [sic] Is Always Red.*

The sign always blinks and is neon.
The flies in the window are dead.
The salad is always cole slaw.
And the Jello is always red.

Lime Jello Marshmallow Cottage Cheese Surprise: The Recipe

Here's an interpretation of the dish celebrated in William Bolcom's song.

1 (3-ounce) package lime Jell-O gelatin
1 cup boiling water
1 (20-ounce) can crushed pineapple, undrained
1 cup cottage cheese
1/2 cup whipped cream or Cool Whip
1/4 cup pecans, chopped
1 (4-ounce) jar maraschino cherries, drained
1 cup miniature marshmallows
2 slices of pimento
15 to 20 sugar wafers
1 (8-ounce) can pineapple rings
Mayonnaise

Dissolve Jell-O in boiling water. Drain crushed pineapple, reserving 1/2 cup of syrup. Add that syrup to gelatin. Chill until thickened but not set (about 1 hour). Fold in pineapple, cottage cheese, whipped cream, pecans, cherries, marshmallows, and pimento. Pour into 5-cup mold. Chill until set (at least 4 hours). Unmold onto plate. Decorate edges of plate with sugar wafers. Decorate top with pineapple rings and mayonnaise. Serves 9.

Gesner's lyrical exploration of a diner menu's sameness continues for three more verses before it concludes:

I don't ask for a millionaire's menu
Or to dine in an elegant hall,
Just a place where the Jello is yellow,
Or maybe—no Jello at all.

Although Gesner likes this song, he says it does not reflect his own largely positive feelings about a dessert that at

A scene from Clark Gesner's "The Jello Is Always Red"

least indirectly helped launch his life as a writer. The credit should actually probably go to a diner waitress who once tried to sell him and his family riced (or flaked) Jell-O under the incorrect, misleading, and not-very-appealing name Rice Jell-O.

Gesner was nine years old at the time but he says his initial reluctance to order this beautiful dessert based on her mistake taught him a valuable lesson about "the importance of using precisely the right word."

Jiggly Journal

In spring 1992, the *Journal of Irreproducible Results* (*JIR*), a science humor magazine now known as the *Annals of Improbable Research*, published a special issue in honor of what it called "nature's most perfect substance."

One of the eight papers listed, "Attaining Uniform Distribution of Canned Fruit in Jell-O by Isoelectric Focusing Electrophoresis," featured a photo of some electrical equipment next to a tub of unpeeled fruit floating in Jell-O water. The experiment used the electric field normally employed to activate proteins and nucleic acids to move fruit in Jell-O. While the results were generally successful, "an empty zone was found in the lime Jell-O where no fruit migrated; in fact, we sensed a reluctance on the part of all the fruits to migrate into the lime Jell-O, an opinion shared by many humans . . ."

Like many other great scientific advances, including Post-it notes and penicillin, Jell-O's

efficacy as a book preservative was discovered by accident—in this case by a sloppy librarian who was reading while eating, noted Nouleigh Rhee Furbished in his paper "Preserving Books with Jell-O." After carefully studying this and other gelatin book stains, Furbished and his colleagues in the preservation office of the Molesworth Institute concluded that Jell-O neutralizes acid and strengthens fibers in paper about twice as well as unflavored, uncolored gelatin.

"At first we considered trying to match the color of the Jell-O to the title or text of the book (i.e., *The Red Badge of Courage*), but we eventually concluded that yellow Jell-O . . . not only preserves our collection but allows us to advertise it as pre-highlighted for the discriminating reader."

Other papers explained how Jell-O killed the dinosaurs and has been used as housing insulation.

Later that year *JIR* confirmed its commitment to Jell-O by awarding General Foods USA technical supervisor Ivette Bassa one of its Ig Nobel Prizes for scientific achievements that "can not or should not be reproduced" for "her role in the crowning achievement of twentieth century chemistry, the synthesis of bright blue Jell-O."

Pop Art on a Plate

Much of '60s pop art explored America's obsession with everyday, commercial products. Claes Oldenburg, in particular, was famous for soft sculpture ice-cream cones, hamburgers, and cake. Critics at the time said the soft texture humanized the objects and forced

Pop artist Claes Oldenburg's molds

people to think about them as something more than just food stuff.

This was even more literally true of the Jell-O casts Oldenburg made from a mold of his own face. The so-called Life Cast plaster mask was made for Oldenburg in 1966 by Michael Kirby, an author and performance artist who himself once consumed a white chocolate hand during a performance.

Over the next few years Oldenburg exhibited and invited gallery goers to eat gelatin casts made from this mold. At Oldenburg's 1968 Los Angeles show, the gelatin faces were smashed—whether by art or food critics no one knows.

Face Job   You, too, can make like famous pop artist Claes Oldenburg and cast your own image in Jell-O with the help of Michael Samonek's Eat Yer Face Gelatin Mold Kit.

"The Ultimate in Personalized Gifts—YOU!" "Cannibal fun for everyone!" reads mold kit promotional copy that hints of Samonek's advertising copywriter day job. By night the suburban Cleveland resident sells novelty products like chocolate perfume and cookbooks that explain how to make glow-in-the-dark gelatin molds, among other "special effect" recipes.

The Eat Yer Face Gelatin Mold Kit was inspired—not by Claes Oldenburg—but by the mail-order novelty products businessman who told Samonek that his

best-sellers were a brain gelatin mold and anything that could be personalized. "I realized that something combining those two ideas could be a hit," Samonek said.

An amazing number of people have, in fact, paid him $19.95 for the privilege of having their face covered in dental plaster while breathing through straws that have been jammed up their nose. To answer the obvious questions: Yes, the kit can be used to mold other body parts, and no, face cloning should not be attempted by anyone with claustrophobic tendencies. "They freak out," he says.

Samonek's four pages of single-space instructions also include a recipe for flesh-toned gelatin to pour into the mold. If frozen, the mold itself "can be used over and over again for different occasions throughout the year" (although it's hard to think of that many occasions where it *would* be appropriate).

Most people serve them at parties. Here's customer Deborah Trimmer's experience doing that, as reported on Samonek's Web site (www.specialeffectscookbook.com): "When we walked into the room with our two lime-green gelatin faces on a serving platter and invited our guests to take a bite out of us, the place went nuts. They're still talking about it almost a year later!"

Hearing nice stuff like that, Samonek says, "I kind of get a catch in my throat," (although we're wondering if it might not just be a piece of stray dental plaster).

Some jiggling Jell-O launches one of the most suspenseful stalk-and-chase scenes in *Jurassic Park*. The kids Tim and Lex had narrowly escaped death by dinosaur several times when scientist Alan Grant leaves them in the supposedly safe visitor's center. But only when the siblings go into the center's cafeteria to eat and Lex's Jell-O suddenly starts jiggling on her spoon does it dawn on her that *they* could end up being the snack.

One thing Alex Portnoy does not complain about in Philip Roth's 1969 novel *Portnoy's Complaint* is his mother. "My mother . . . could accomplish anything . . . ," he says early in the novel, citing as proof her ability to "make Jell-O . . . with sliced peaches HANGING in it, just SUSPENDED there, in defiance of the law of gravity."

In the 1959 comedy classic *Some Like It Hot*, an admiring Jack Lemmon describes Marilyn Monroe as moving "like Jell-O on springs!"

Dan Aykroyd takes one look at a museum covered with the evil slime in the movie *Ghostbusters 2* and says, "It looks like a giant Jell-O mold." "I hate Jell-O," replies Ernie Hudson. But Bill Murray rushes to Jell-O's defense with the familiar, "Oh come on, there's always room for Jell-O."

In *My Best Friend's Wedding*, Julia Roberts uses Jell-O to explain why her friend Michael has called off his wedding with Kimmy Wallace (Cameron Diaz). It's as if Michael has gone to a fancy French restaurant and ordered crème brûlée—but then decided he would really much rather have humble Jell-O. "He's comfortable with Jell-O," Roberts explains. "I realize compared to crème brûlée it's Jell-O but maybe that's what he needs." Then "I have to be Jell-O!" Kimmy cries.

In Woody Allen's 1966 play *Don't Drink the Water*, Walter Hollander, a "creative caterer" from Newark, is mistaken for a spy while on vacation in an unnamed communist country. While there, he tells embassy officials he was "the first to make bridegrooms out of potato salad" and once "did the bride's body in Jell-O, her head in a very nice clam dip, with fruit punch spouting out of her throat."

Jell-O is one of the foods Mickey Rourke feeds a blindfolded Kim Basinger in the steamy refrigerator scene of the 1985 movie *9 $^1/_2$ Weeks*.

Chevy Chase gags on a lime Jell-O mold an elderly aunt brings for dinner in *National Lampoon's Christmas Vacation*. "Does your cat by any chance eat Jell-O?" he asks Aunt Bethany as the camera pans to the cat food mold decoration.

The short-lived 1999 film *Body Shots* was originally called *Jello* [sic] *Shots* until Kraft trademark attorneys found out it was about a night of drunken debauchery fueled by Jell-O shots. In the movie the shots are served on huge trays by pillbox hat–adorned waitresses in aerial views so arty they make June Taylor routines look like halftime at a junior high football game.

Jell-O is one of the more frightening aspects of human civilization encountered by the alien investigation team headed by John Lithgow on the TV comedy *Third Rock From the Sun*.

When alien officer Sally Solomon and intelligence specialist Tommy get their first look at a wobbling lime Jell-O mold, they try to kill it by stabbing it with a knife and stuffing it down the sink. And when the aliens' landlady brings in a Jell-O mold as the crowning treat of their first Thanksgiving feast, the aliens scream and run for cover.

"If the Chrysler Building Were a Jell-O Mold," is one of a series of great-buildings-as-desserts illustrator Dave Jonason did for *Frankfurter Allgemeine* (more or less the German equivalent of the *New York Times Magazine*). Jonason also drew the Taj Mahal as an ice-cream sundae, the Parthenon as a wedding cake, and Stonehenge as shortbread cookies.

In Louise Erdrich's 1986 novel *The Beet Queen*, Celestine James gets revenge on Jell-O-making friend Mary Adare by bringing a Jell-O salad filled with nuts and bolts to a potluck in Mary's name.

In the 1996 novel *Playing the Bones*, a blues musician pulls a gun on someone over whether Jell-O is really salad or dessert. Later that question becomes a metaphor for the book's heroine of large appetites—a woman with two lovers from two different worlds who wants "Jell-O to be both salad and dessert."

The Jell-O Syndrome was a 1986 young adult novel and that novel's derogatory term for girls who have Jell-O for brains (i.e., spend all their time mooning over boys). We don't know why the novel's name was later changed to *The Problem With Love* but we wouldn't be surprised if Kraft trademark attorneys had something to do with it. Maybe they didn't read all the way to the end of the novel when the heroine realizes that "what I had called the Jell-Os was sometimes a very good thing, sensitivity maybe, or a willingness to feel things deeply."

"He had a broad face and a little round belly, / That shook when he laughed like a bowlful of jelly." Most people reading this line from *A Visit from St. Nicholas* today assume Clement Moore was comparing Santa's shaking belly to the jelly we spread on bread. But when Moore wrote this Christmas classic in 1822, sweet gelatin desserts were widely known by the English term, jelly. When was the last time you saw toast jelly truly shake, anyway?

In Alfred Hitchcock's *Psycho*, investigator Arbogast expresses his skepticism about Norman Bates's initial answers to his questions about the missing Marion Crane (Janet Leigh) by saying, "You see, if it doesn't jell, it isn't aspic. And this ain't jelling. It's not coming together." In director Gus Van Sant's 1998 remake, the word aspic was changed to Jell-O.

In 1982, a humor book called *Real Men Don't Eat Quiche* was climbing best-seller lists. One of the last scenes in the Arnold Schwarzenegger movie *Kindergarten Cop* recalls this book as it pokes fun at Jell-O. Detective John Kimble is in the hospital after the big shoot-out, being spoon-fed Jell-O by a nurse when John's crime-fighting partner, Phoebe O'Hara (Pamela Reed), walks into his room and puts a stop to it. "He doesn't want to eat that. He's a tough guy. Tough guys don't eat Jell-O," she chides.

TV's *The Pretender* stars Jarod Russell as a genius raised in isolation so he doesn't know about the simplest things. In each episode he assumes a new identity and discovers some new product of American commercial culture. In the first episode of 1998, that product was Jell-O. "It's a dessert. You got it in the lunch line at school, remember?" explains a messmate at the Army Training Center where Russell is posing as a soldier to get to the bottom of a Vietnam War injustice.

Later he eats Jell-O while doing some computer research. The episode ends with a corrupt officer stepping on a fake land mine Russell has planted that produces "blood" made of you-know-what. "Don't wet your pants, sir. It's Jell-O. It's a dessert. It's yummy," he mocks.

The Piccadilly Cafeteria restaurant chain boasts of "50 feet of hot, wholesome home-style cookin'" But their 1999 advertising campaign focused on the one and a half feet devoted to blue Jell-O. Billboards read simply, "We've got blue Jell-O." TV ads showed kids peering through blue Jell-O cubes. "It's a great hook for kids," said Danny Mitchell of Piccadilly's advertising agency. "And . . . if the place has got blue Jell-O, what does that say about how much else they have . . . ?"

"Look mom, they've got Blue Jello!" PICCADILLY — Who Says You Can't Please Everybody.

In 2000, ESPN used a hockey player's Jell-O fantasy to promote its coverage of the Stanley Cup Playoffs. As the TV spot begins, Dallas Stars center Joe Nieuwendyk wheels an

A Stanley Cup Jell-O mold

upside-down Stanley Cup on a cart into a roomful of people seated for a fancy dinner. Then Nieuwendyk starts wacking at the Cup with a wooden mallet. "What are you doing?" someone at the table asks just before the lime gelatin mold plops out. There's laughter and applause, then these words: "Who will win it this year? What will they do with it?"

Judy Weiss (left) in the costume she wore to the 1985 Myth California Counter-Pageant held outside the Miss California pageant in Santa Cruz to protest some of the beautifying techniques employed by beauty contestants. Her costume lives on in the form of a postcard distributed by the Media Watch media literacy organization.

Mexican artist César Martínez uses 220 pounds of peach Jell-O mixed with milk to make gelatin replicas of life-size reclining nude men that are the focal point of his political performance art pieces. The Jell-O man he brought to the Corcoran Gallery of Art in Washington, D.C., in 1996 was meant to symbolize Mexicans hurt by the North American Free Trade Agreement. "This is the blood and corpse of the last immigrant," Martínez told the Corcoran crowd before slicing off a foot and inviting the crowd to partake.

A patron of the arts partakes of the Jell-O man.

Chapter 9

JELL-O FANS

*J*ell-O-brand gelatin is one of the most familiar products in America. In the late 1990s, 99 percent of Americans could identify it, which is more than the percentage who could identify Bill Clinton or Al Gore.

At some point during one year, 75 percent of all American homes will have at least one box of Jell-O in the cupboard. This same percentage of Americans buys about 312 million packages of Jell-O gelatin per year. That's ten boxes of Jell-O per second or eighty Jell-O boxes sliding across check-out scanners since you started reading this sentence.

Although this is not as impressive a statement as it was when cake mixes were the height of convenience, Jell-O is nevertheless still America's most popular prepared dessert.

Thanksgiving Sampler

Thanksgiving is D-day for Jell-O molds. (That's *D* as in a Jell-O mold is *delicious* with turkey.) Like to start this tradition in your family but don't know what recipe to use?

Here are a few options. The black cherry one is similar to one made by Liza Ashley, former cook for Bill Clinton when he was Arkansas governor. The classic Cranberry Jell-O Waldorf Salad is a favorite of Jell-O collector Marilyn Felling. The relish is a holiday tradition handed down to a friend by her maternal grandmother, Mildred Joyce Hobson.

Bill's Bing Cherry Salad

1 (15-ounce) can pitted dark sweet cherries in juice

1 (3-ounce) package cherry Jell-O gelatin

1 cup boiling water

2 tablespoons lemon juice

Cold water

$^1/_4$ to $^1/_2$ cup walnuts (optional)

Drain can of cherries and reserve juice. Dissolve Jell-O in hot water. Combine reserved cherry juice, lemon juice, and enough cold water to equal 1 cup, then add to Jell-O. Refrigerate until slightly set. Add cherries and nuts, then pour into 4-cup mold. Chill until firm. Serves 6.

JELL-O Cranberry Waldorf Salad Mold

1 $^1/_2$ cups boiling water

1 (6-ounce) package cranberry Jell-O gelatin

1 (16-ounce) can whole cranberry sauce

1 cup cold water

$^1/_2$ teaspoon ground cinnamon

1 medium apple, chopped and peeled (Granny Smith is best)

$^3/_4$ cup diced celery

$^3/_4$ cup chopped walnuts or pecans

Stir boiling water into gelatin in large bowl for 2 minutes or until completely dissolved. Stir in cranberry sauce, cold water and cinnamon. Refrigerate about 1 $^1/_2$ hours or until thickened (when a spoon drawn through leaves a definite impression.)

Stir in apple, celery, and nuts. Spoon into 5-cup mold. Refrigerate 4 hours or until firm. Unmold. Serves 10.

Cranberry Orange JELL-O Relish

2 (12-ounce) bags fresh cranberries

2 oranges, including rinds

1 (3-ounce) package of Jell-O gelatin, any red flavor

1 cup boiling water

1 cup sugar

2 apples, diced

4 stalks of celery, diced

1 (16-ounce) bag of walnuts, broken into small pieces

Place cranberries and whole oranges in a meat grinder or blender and grind into small pieces. Dissolve Jell-O in water, then add sugar and rest of ingredients. Mix thoroughly. Pour into dish, cover, and place in refrigerator for at least 2 hours. Serves 4 to 6.

About 80 percent of all Jell-O use is everyday snacking and dessert eating. So why do most people associate it with holidays and other family celebrations? Because Jell-O does, in fact, experience sales spikes around Thanksgiving, Christmas, Easter, and Halloween.

Among those contributing to that spike in Thanksgiving 1993 were Bill and Hillary Clinton, who continued a long tradition of Jell-O eating in the White House by serving a bing cherry Jell-O mold. Woodrow Wilson reportedly ended his first day in office enjoying a dessert made with gelatin, custard, and whipped cream. In 1990, an assistant chef at the White House embarrassed his colleagues in the pastry shop by serving the first set of Bushes an orange Jell-O pie, according to papers from an employment discrimination case suit filed after he was let go.

United States of JELL-O

Sales figures confirm Jell-O's status as our unofficial state food. They're strong all over America but most robust in the midwestern heartland. In fact, three of the fifteen points in the "Midwestern Bill of Rights" drafted by the author of the book *Calling the Midwest Home* at least indirectly involve Jell-O. They are the right to "consume a meal that is entirely composed of pale food" (i.e., lemon Jell-O), the right to "prepare molded salads with any food item that will fit on either a spoon or fork," and the right to "recognize haute cuisine" but "prefer low."

As for specifically where in the Midwest Jell-O sells the best: it depends on when you ask. In 1989, it was Grand Rapids, Michigan, a city previously distinguished for its record-breaking rat poison sales.

But in the early '90s, Salt Lake City,

Gelatin: A World Tour

"Jell-O is an all-American product" is not just some half-jelled idea. That's not just because Jell-O was invented in North America but also because the North American continent is about the only place it's sold and known.

Jell-O has been made and sold in Canada almost as long as in the United States. For the most part, Canadian products and advertising have mirrored efforts here. One notable exception is a Fantasy Flavors line introduced in the '60s that included root beer, bubble gum, and cinnamon-flavored gelatins. Pear, honeydew melon, and orange julep have also been sold there.

Canada's split identity is also reflected in Jell-O culture. In line with the country's British roots, gelatin there is called jelly powder. And yet Jell-O sells best in the French-speaking province of Quebec, where people apparently get endless amusement out of Jell-O's similarity to the French phrase, *J'ai l'eau,* as in *J'ai l'eau à la bouche* (My mouth is watering).

Gelatin box in Arabic

Jell-O is also sold in Mexico although gelatin's popularity there goes well beyond the modest sales of Jell-O (one of the few brands sold in boxes instead of pouches). In Mexico gelatin desserts containing fruit and parfait layers are popular snacks you can purchase by the cup from street vendors or by the mold slice in delis and bakeries. Mexicans can go to these same bakeries to order specially decorated birthday or anniversary molds—the same way North Americans order birthday or anniversary cakes.

Maria de Lourdes Sobrino of LuLu's Mexican dessert company in Vernon, California, says slices of birthday cakes in Mexico are traditionally served alongside a slice of gelatin mold instead of the scoop of ice cream you'd get in the United States. Perhaps not coincidentally, in Mexico gelatin is frequently prepared with milk or cream instead of water and comes in flavors most Americans would associate with ice cream or pudding (like chocolate, vanilla, and pistachio) as well as fruit ones.

Gelatin is popular in virtually all Latin countries. Gelatin marketers theorize it's because of Latins' love of fruit flavors and sweets, and a climate that favors light desserts.

Another growing market for gelatin is in the Asian Pacific. Food companies in Japan and Taiwan are way ahead of U.S. manufacturers in gelatin convenience judging from the coffee creamer–size grab-and-gulp seaweed-based snacks they sell in litchi and coconut as well as more familiar fruit flavors.

Citizens of Great Britain and its former colonies enjoy gelatin desserts in much the same way as Americans except that the "jelly" is sold in meltable blocks as well as in crystals. Roundtree, Angel Delight, and Tesco are some of the big brand names. In Australia you can buy flavors such as port wine and quandong (a rainforest fruit). A popular brand called Aeroplane sells one of the only lines of naturally flavored and colored gelatins. Australia is also where the world's record for the largest single batch of gelatin was set in 1981: 7,700 gallons of pink watermelon gelatin made in a swimming pool in Brisbane. Watermelon was chosen by a sponsoring radio station as the perfect medium for black plastic "seeds"—really numbered disks— they let listeners jump in to retrieve for corresponding prizes. Grand prize was the swimming pool (presumably without the gelatin).

Central and East European chefs typically use sheets of unflavored gelatin to make savory aspics. Russians would likewise traditionally use gelatin to encase pigs' feet or other meats. But gelatin is proving to be one of the more easily transferable aspects of democracy. At least that was Shannon Lucid's experience on Mir (see Chapter 7) and London-based French chef Michel Roux's belief after cooking for President Boris Yeltsin in 1994. Although Roux was given a free hand to come up with his menu of caviar, foie gras, beef Beaujolais, French cheeses, and an apple tart, nervous Russian chefs supplemented his efforts at the last minute with sure-to-please bowls of Jell-O.

South-of-the-Border-Style Gelatin

Here's how to make a Mexican-style creamy gelatin with American-style Jell-O.

1 (3-ounce) package Jell-O gelatin, any flavor
1 cup boiling water
1 cup milk, not too cold

Stir boiling water into Jell-O until completely dissolved. Let cool to room temperature. Add milk. Refrigerate 4 hours or until firm. Serves 4.

Utah, residents became the Jell-O-buying champs by eating four boxes per person per year, or about four times as much as the average American. Local food experts attribute this to the city's extensive Mormon population with their large families and low alcohol consumption, and compensating high sugar intake. Salt Lake City residents also buy more lime Jell-O than all other Americans (presumably to make that most popular of local Jell-O dishes, lime Jell-O with shredded carrots).

Food Fight

Then, in 1999, Kraft literally shook the Jell-O-eating world by announcing that Des Moines, Iowa, had

Preston A. Daniels, Robin Heinemann, and Dave Feehan at the Des Moines' Metropolitan Mayor's Ball

wrestled the Jell-O consumption title away from Salt Lake. Des Moines Mayor Preston Daniels marked the milestone by handing out plastic Jell-O molds shaped like "2000" at his black-tie New Year's millennial ball, and even allowed a local newspaper reporter to make a Jell-O mold of his face.

To demonstrate Utahns' greater love for Jell-O (and also, not coincidentally, to promote public TV's *The Red Green Show*), fund-raisers at the Salt Lake City public television station asked viewers to send

boxes of green Jell-O to Iowa Public Television. (Within a week, Friends of Iowa Public Television director Rich Adamson received 201 boxes.)

A couple of months later, Scott Blackerby of Salt Lake's Bambara risked his restaurant's upscale

reputation by launching a "Take Back the Title!" Jell-O recipe contest, reasoning that "The more people experiment with their recipes, . . . the more Jell-O gelatin they'll buy," and the greater the chance Utah could recapture the Jell-O capital title. The winning entry was a yellow-

Scott Blackerby of Bambara

green beehive-shaped Jell-O mold containing plastic dinosaurs, a cricket, and photos of twelve Utah governors (among other symbols of Utah history and culture). The top children's prize went to a plate of Jell-O decorated with drips of marshmallow creme

A Winner of 2000 Bambara Salt Lake City Jell-O Contest

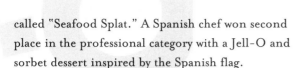

called "Seafood Splat." A Spanish chef won second place in the professional category with a Jell-O and sorbet dessert inspired by the Spanish flag.

Gourmet Jell-O dishes like Mint Cream Dream and Bavarian Creamsicle Jell-O were also featured on Bambara's dessert menu throughout that spring and summer. Thanks in part to Blackerby's efforts, Utah regained the Jell-O eating crown in early 2001. To celebrate, Bill Cosby delivered a free comedy routine to a joint session of the Utah state legislature, which rewarded him by making Jell-O the state's official snack food (although one senator did wonder aloud if Jell-O might not have too much "wiggle and jiggle" for such a wholesome state).

State of Lime

Jell-O activity in Utah long predates the recent lost title drama. Both Salt Lake newspapers have sponsored Jell-O cooking contests and acknowledged the local population's love of lime with special "green" categories. In 1998, the winner of *Deseret News*'s contest was Big Blue Marble, a depiction of the earth sculpted from berry blue Jell-O and whipped cream and featuring dry ice clouds. Its creator—the president of a local Ladies of the Bible Luncheon Club—told judges it was inspired by Genesis.

And you won't find any corned beef and cabbage or green beer at Flanigan's in Zion National Park on St. Patrick's Day. Instead, this Irish restaurant and inn celebrates the holiday with a lime Jell-O

This Shakes, Rattles, and Spews

The top prizewinner in the Red Green division of Bambara restaurant's 2000 Jell-O recipe contest was an active green Jell-O volcano. Here's one way to make your own.

6 (8-inch) baked round cakes
Brown and green frosting
1 (3-ounce) package Jell-O gelatin, any flavor
1 (8-ounce) bottle lemon juice
1 tablespoon baking soda

Construct a cake volcano by trimming the cake layers in successively smaller rounds and stacking them on a large platter. Remove top two layers. Using a small, short juice or shot glass as a tool, carefully make a hole in the center of the top two layers that is as tall or taller than the glass. Replace layers onto the volcano and frost the entire cake in chocolate, smoothing out the stacking steps. Decorate the cake with green frosting to resemble trees and other vegetation. Line the hole with foil.

Prepare Jell-O according to package directions. Let cool 15 minutes. Fill half juice glass with warm (not hot) Jell-O. Pour in lemon juice so that mixture comes to $1/2$ inch from the glass top. Place glass into hole in the cake. Gather your audience, then put 1 tablespoon of baking soda into the glass and stir briefly. Jell-O "lava" will pour out the top of the glass and down the cake sides. Edible for up to 30 people.

sculpting contest. Notable recent entries have included Mount KillamaJell-O, "Jell-Oassic Park," and a painting by MichaelanJell-O.

Utah even has its own Jell-O mold building—and unlike Seattle's, it's still standing. The owners of Salt

Lake City's Grunts and Postures vintage clothing store originally nailed about 100 Jell-O molds to the front and side of their building to protect it from graffiti. Now their problem is mold theft.

Salt Lake City's Grunts and Postures

And guess which of the hundreds of Olympic pin designs issued by the 2002 Salt Lake organizing committee has sold best? That's right, it's the one depicting a bowl of cubed lime gelatin now only available on the secondary collectors market for a cool $150 to $200 each.

Craig Weston of pin maker Aminco International says his company's California-based executives initially dismissed the idea of a Jell-O pin, reasoning

that most "states would be embarrassed" to be known as the Jell-O-eating capital of the world. But Utahns "are very proud of it," Aminco vice president David Hyman soon discovered when they snapped up the first three thousand lime Jell-O pins, and a subsequent one featuring lime Jell-O and shredded carrots in a matter of weeks.

Manna for Mormans

Utahns' love of low-brow cooking was also the inspiration for Roger B. Salazar and Michael G. Wightman's *No Man Knows My Pastries*, a humorous cookbook that has become a smash hit for Salt Lake City's Signature Books. The book was supposedly written by Sister Enid Christensen, described in the book's biography as "a prominent leader in the Payson, Utah, 227th (Mormon) Ward Relief Society" (really Salazar in drag), and features real if equally unlikely looking recipes for Sin-O-Men Rolls, Pearl of Great Spice, and Tuna à la King of Kings. The book is filled with both Biblical in-jokes and convenience foods. Jell-O gets its own

From No Man Knows My Pastries

The Jell-O Belt

chapter and a chart matching Jell-O molds to common Mormon social occasions.

"If you ask a Mormon to bring a green salad to a potluck, they will bring green Jell-O," said Salazar when asked to explain the book's inspiration.

Jell-O is also worshiped in Lutheran churches in Minnesota and the Dakotas, if you take what Garrison Keillor says about it on *A Prairie Home Companion* seriously (and you probably shouldn't). Janet Martin also pokes gentle fun at the dessert in her *Lutheran Church Basement Women* cookbook (which comes with or without its companion Lutheran Jell-O Power apron). The book's Jell-O chapter is subdivided by color and includes recipes for "Everyday Jell-O" (the box instructions) and "Jell-O for a Crowd" (those instructions times four). Martin is also coauthor of a study of Catholic–Lutheran relations entitled *They Glorified Mary . . . We Glorified Rice.* (For all those with limited church supper experience, Glorified Rice is a dish made by combining Jell-O with fruit juice, cooked rice, and whipped cream.)

Glorified Rice

A church potluck favorite that's truly heaven sent.

1 (3-ounce) package lemon Jell-O gelatin
1 cup boiling water
1 cup canned pineapple juice
1/2 teaspoon salt
2 cups cold cooked rice
4 tablespoons sugar
1 cup heavy cream, whipped

Dissolve Jell-O in boiling water. Add pineapple juice and salt. Chill. When slightly thickened, beat mixture until the consistency of whipped cream. Fold rice into Jell-O. Add sugar to whipped cream and then add whipped cream into Jell-O. Turn into mold. Chill until firm. Serves 8.

In a much more (too?) serious vein is 2000's *Whitebread Protestants*, a study of food and religion in which author and minister Daniel Sack confirms the essential truth of the joke about the schoolchildren who participated in a show-and-tell about their religious heritages.

"I'm Jewish and this is a Star of David," the first child says. "I'm Catholic and this is a crucifix," says the next. "I'm Protestant and this is a Jell-O mold," says the last. In fact, Sack argues that in many Protestant congregations, sitting down together to eat Jell-O salads is even more important to building religious community than worship services!

On the Menu

You don't have to be religious to find Jell-O.

Nonbelievers seeking its comforts need look no further than the nearest diner, deli, or cafeteria.

Jell-O is so much a part of these places as to have its own lexicon. "Shivering Liz," "shimmy," or "nervous pudding" are a few of the ways it's referred to.

If you hear one of these phrases ring out at a deli in New York City at eight some morning, don't think you heard wrong. You've probably just stumbled into the place where talk show host Sally Jessy Raphael goes every morning to get her breakfast Jell-O. (Anyone who knows about Raphael's trademark glasses won't have to ask the color Jell-O she orders.)

Jell-O is even bigger in institutional settings or programs, 94 percent of which serve it regularly, according to a 1998 survey by *FoodService Director* magazine.

Yes, schools still serve it. In fact, Julie Sprekelmeyer of ARAMARK says that gelatin is probably the third most popular dessert served in the 350 school cafeterias her food service company manages (after cookies and pudding), and that it is typically offered once or twice a week in elementary schools and practically every day as part of salad bars in junior high and high schools.

A 1999 attempt to wean students at the University of California at Berkeley off their twelve-hundred-servings-a-week Jell-O habit was met with a flood of protest. Dining service director Nancy Jurich says she was only trying to introduce more variety into her dessert menu. But she's learned her lesson. (Jurich now even goes to the trouble of serving Jell-O cubes in the school colors of blue and yellow during school orientation.)

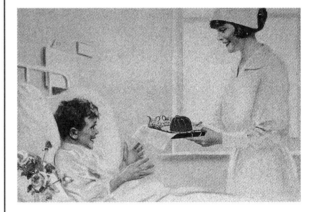

Bouncy Balm

Rare is the hospital patient who is not served Jell-O. It's offered to everyone from expectant women to heart transplant patients, mainly because it meets the requirements of almost every kind of restricted diet. Jell-O's ability to morph from solid to liquid at mouth

MISTER BOFF

PEOPLE UNCLEAR ON THE CONCEPT

© 1996 Joe Martin, Inc./Dist. by Universal Press Syndicate

E mail: mrboffo@mrboffo.com

temperature is the reason. Plus, sick people really like it.

"Patients who haven't eaten anything for a while get really excited about . . . anything they can chew," says Georgetown University Hospital nutritionist Donna Runyan. "It's like, 'Oh, boy! Jell-O!'" And let's face it: Jell-O is a gourmet treat compared to an IV. Runyan says Jell-O is also a kind of comfort food because it reminds people of what their mommies used to give them when they were home sick from school.

And unlike butter for burns, Jell-O is still doctor recommended for upset stomachs, sore throats, diarrhea, and losing some excess poundage (for the last two, Sugar Free is usually preferred).

Sugar Free Jell-O is a zero points food on the Weight Watchers program, meaning that people can eat as much of it as they want. It's actually one of the few foods that contains fewer calories than it burns up to digest. No wonder Sugar Free Jell-O now captures 40 percent of Jell-O gelatin sales. One

by Joe Martin

How to Eat JELL-O Like a Child

(WITH APOLOGIES TO DELIA EPHRON)

Squish it back and forth between your teeth, as noisily as possible, until it becomes a liquid. Spit the liquid at your brother.

Slurp it up with a straw, then blow it into somebody's face.

With a knife, create narrow roadways in your Jell-O to the fruit. Put some ants on the top and see if they crawl down the tunnels.

Wait until your sister is eating her Jell-O, then make her laugh.

Watch her nose in hopes the Jell-O will come out of it.

Don't use a spoon or your hands. Just put your face in the bowl and suck it up.

Throw Jell-O at the ceiling and see if it sticks.

Wet a finger, then stick it into the packet of Jell-O sugar and eat it plain.

Put Jell-O cubes on flat plates and try to scoop them up with a spoon without using your fingers. Make this into a race.

Carve mountains out of Jell-O, then simulate an avalanche by pouring milk or light cream over the top.

If you have a block of Jell-O on a plate, shake the plate so that it wobbles. Eventually shake it hard enough that it launches.

See how high you can make a Jell-O cube bounce off your spoon.

Construct a Jell-O cube tower or building.

Wobble some Jell-O and tell your baby sister that it's alive. Tell older kids that it is shaking because it is afraid of you.

If having Jell-O salad, mix it into your potatoes to make them pink.

If there's some Jell-O in the refrigerator and no adults are at home, spread the Jell-O on the floor and slide around in it in your bare feet. Or empty it in the bathtub, take off your clothes, and sit in it.

What price JELL-O collectibles?

Given Jell-O's popularity with collectors, might that something-Jell-O you have kicking around your attic be able to fund your kid's college career?

Not likely.

One of the reasons Jell-O is such a popular collectible is that Jell-O stuff is so available and affordable. Between 1925 and 1930, for instance, the company sent out about a million aluminum Jell-O molds to consumers who paid the minimal shipping and handling fee. Because of their durability and wide availability, these same molds are today only worth about $1 to $5 each. Newer, plastic Jiggler molds are worth even less.

Ditto for Jell-O paper collectibles. The tiny recipe booklets that were inserted into Jell-O boxes through the '50s, for instance, can now be purchased for $3 to $10 each. The larger recipe booklets that the company distributed by the millions through the '30s are generally worth $15 to $30; Jell-O magazine ads, $8 to $10 each.

The exceptions are paper materials

from Jell-O's very earliest years or cross-collectibles (items that hit two or more collecting interests). Jell-O recipe books illustrated by Norman Rockwell or Maxfield Parrish or featuring comic Jack Benny, for instance, are worth from two to three times the figures just cited. Four L. Frank Baum booklets issued in conjunction with a Jell-O-sponsored *Wizard of Oz* radio show (and printed on flimsy paper) are now worth at least $150 each (although one set of four recently sold for $1,600). Perfect examples of some of the baseball cards printed on the backs of Jell-O boxes in the early '60s are worth $500 each (in part because so few kids cut straight!).

Jell-O silver and dishware offered as premiums or given away at fairs fall into the middle price range. Jell-O spoons featuring the Jell-O Girl can be had for $25 to $75. Because they're breakable and fewer have survived, Jell-O dishes and china plates fetch more like $200 each.

The most valuable Jell-O collectibles are also the most fragile. These are hand-painted Sebastian Miniature figurines made in the '50s and given out to grocery distributors to alert them to new Jell-O advertising. Since only 3,000 of each figure were made, and since Sebastians are highly collectible in and of themselves, collectors who are able to find one of these are generally happy to pay $400 or $500 each. A ceramic cow creamer with fruit on its sides but no direct mention of Jell-O offered to Jell-O consumers for $1 at

about the same time is now worth $300 to $400.

Tops on serious Jell-O collectors' wish lists are turn-of-the-twentieth-century Jell-O store signs and displays. In 1996, one of those collectors proved it by paying $3,100 for a three-part cardboard store window display showing a little girl preparing a dessert that then sold for a mere 10 cents.

Jell-O dieting success story is actor John Malkovich, who as a high school student lost seventy pounds in six months on an all-Jell-O diet.

JELL-Oabelia

Jell-O is not just popular as something to eat. It's also a popular collectible.

Bob Andes, a Jell-O collector and a contributor to the *Vintage Cookbooks and Advertising Leaflets* price guide, believes there are hundreds of active Jell-O collectors; others believe there could be as many as one thousand. Despite this, there are no Jell-O fan clubs or collectors' conventions as there are for Pez and Star Trek.

"There's too much rivalry," Andes explained. "What would happen if a dealer showed up with a rare piece . . . ?" he said with a verbal shudder, leaving you to imagine the details of the bloody battle.

One of Andes's most famous Jell-O collecting rivals lives right near Kraft headquarters in suburban Chicago—the better to find insider collectibles at local flea markets? Sharon Swartz says no. But the Jell-O-box-adorned hat she wears on her flea market runs to let dealers know what she wants has made her locally famous as "the Jell-O Lady."

Swartz's fame as Jell-O collector rose to new heights when she appeared on Oprah Winfrey's 1997 Mother's Day show—most appropriately since Swartz was inspired to pick up her first Jell-O cookbook by fond memories of making Jell-O with her own mom.

The JELL-O Answer Lady

Jell-O suspenders. Jell-O kites. Jell-O wrestling videotape. Jell-O shots cookbook. Boxes of every flavor and every brand of gelatin sold in China and Japan. A cigarette lighter that plays the Jell-O theme song.

Marilyn Felling has all this and so much more that her Grand Junction, Colorado, house includes an all-Jell-O room. In addition to display cases filled with Jell-O molds and boxes, it includes file drawers of Jell-O paper collectibles that she (as unofficial technical consultant to the Jellophile Web site) has used to research questions like "Can I make my own Jell-O 1,2,3?" and "How did people get Jell-O to set

Marilyn Felling

before they had refrigerators?" (Felling's answers? Yes, and "It was left in the sink to cool. Gelatin does not need refrigeration to set.") Given her historical bent, it bugs Felling to no end that she does not know the story behind the metal canister she owns that reads "Jell-O treats you to the movies."

Although Felling obtained most of her collection in the conventional flea market—antique dealer—eBay ways, she once drove an hour to charm a supermarket manager out of a Jell-O NASCAR display. "I got three hundred free molds out of that," she says proudly.

The eclectic Felling also collects flying cars, airplane barf bags, and anything having to do with Kraft's famous processed cheese loaf, Velveeta. But Jell-O is the collection people relate to most readily and enthusiastically.

Artists' Inspiration

Antique dealers trace the popularity of Jell-O collectibles to the beauty of its early advertising booklets.

Saldaña's 3-D rendering of (Jello)³

But it's the beauty of the dessert itself that has attracted the attention of artists like Zoë Sheehan Saldaña.

Saldaña was a master of fine arts student at the Rochester Institute of Technology in 1997 when she decided to create a 3-foot, 2,000-pound Jell-O cube. She made it by mixing 900 6-ounce boxes of strawberry Jell-O with 245 pounds of

Making the Cube

unflavored gelatin in five bottom-opening 50-gallon drums. Because of how long it took to mix each one, she actually had to make the gelatin in 50-gallon batches over the course of five evenings, then refrigerate them so that when the time came to actually pour the stuff into the 3-foot-cube wooden mold she had built, the gelatin had to be melted over butane burners. This took eight hours. Ten cold November days later, the

After two weeks on display

mold was forklifted into Niagara University's Castellani Art Museum and unmolded.

"There was a collective sigh of relief when it stood," recalled Saldaña, despite cracks that grew bigger every day the cube was on display. As for visitor reaction, "People would come in and start laughing. It was as if Martha Stewart had kind of overdid it. The whole gallery smelled of strawberry." After three weeks, though, the smell (from molding) and sagging (from the cracks) got

Sperm/egg: One of Saldaña's smaller creations.

so bad that the cube had to go. Saldaña filled forty garbage bags with its chopped-up remains.

She now does the smallest kind of artwork she could think of although the cause of large-scale Jell-O sculpture has been taken up by Brooklyn-based sculptor Daniel Wurtzel. He's now shopping around a grant proposal to create a gelatin cube more than twice the size of Saldaña's.

Karin Olah was a student in a sculpture class at the Maryland Institute College of Art when she made a Jell-O dress by sewing together Ziploc bags full of Jell-O Jiggler hearts. The dress was meant to

Karin Olah's dress

artistically explore whether there was room in Olah's heart for the two men she was then dating, playing off the advertising assertion that there is "always room for Jell-O."

Pam Larson Kaneb's "Jell-O Drawer" was part of an art show held in and about a friend's Boston apartment. Since the kitchen and bathroom had already been "taken" by other artists, Kaneb borrowed a drawer from Zach Feuer's white platform bed, put a plastic finger puppet in it, then poured in some raspberry Jell-O.

"It had something to do with being a kid; the way kids hide things under beds and in drawers," Kaneb said.

Jell-O was also the inspiration for a mold party a California chapter of the American Institute of Graphic Arts held at the Otis Art Institute in 1985.

Eric Borsum's Matisse-style entry at the Otis Art Institute

Entries included gelatin donuts in a Winchell's box, empty makeup jars refilled with gelatin in appropriate hues, and a splotch of lime Jell-O on a framed slice of white bread entitled "Jell-O Mold." However, grand prize went to the "Granny's Garden Jell-O Recipe," a gelatin mold containing live but cryogenically slowed bugs whose defrosting and escape to freedom was an event highlight.

Teaching Tool

Day care workers and elementary school art teachers commonly use Jell-O to make finger paint, watercolors, and clay they don't have to worry about their charges eating. Jell-O is also the basis of school science lessons on everything from enzymes to optics. Elementary school teachers will wiggle a pan of Jell-O topped with sugar cubes to demonstrate what happens to buildings during an earthquake or pour cooking oil on a blue Jell-O sea to simulate an oil spill.

Other teachers use gelatin brain molds in anatomy classes or to demonstrate the wisdom of wearing bicycle safety helmets. "The kids really love seeing the unprotected ones splatter," says brain mold maker Ken Sibley. Kids in junior high school physics and chemistry classes are asked to test Kraft's assertions that certain fruits will sink in Jell-O while others prevent it from setting—and to figure out why.

One company has even created an optics teaching kit around Jell-O. The Science Source's Edible Optics Study allows students to figure the refraction index and curvature radius of Jell-O lenses before eating them.

The Edible Optics kit

Social Slime

Do you know what's causing school reading scores to soar? At increasing numbers of schools it's the promise of being able to see the principal swim or get dunked in Jell-O. A surprising number of college administrators also use this popular foodstuff to introduce new students to the rigors of college life.

"You feel stupid but everybody feels stupid together," explained Jennifer Carrea, after eating Jell-O without benefit of utensils or hands during freshman orientation at Drew University in 1987.

California principal Lucienne Wong fulfills her promise to swim in Jell-O after her students read 1.5 million pages in six months.

The Utah State Jell-O slide

A Jell-O Slide is a recruiting tool for the Latter Day Saints Men's Association at Utah State University although grown-up organizer Bud Pace says just as many young women as men are attracted to the idea of sliming themselves up in a Jell-O pit, then diving headfirst onto a slick plastic slide. The distance record after eight years: 100 feet.

It's far more common for college administrators to punish students for Jell-O tomfoolery—as when some Queen's University students trapped fellow students in their dorm rooms by pouring Jell-O under their doors. There are shades of *Animal House* in one

Out of the Mouths of Babes Came a Business of Brains
(Not to Mention Hearts, Hands, and Faces)

It all started one day in 1990 when Ken Sibley's five-year-old daughter spotted a fake rubber hand in a store and suggested a Jell-O one would look even more realistic.

Most people would have smiled, nodded, and moved on to the Halloween masks.

But Sheri Sibley's father was an import manager who had seen shoppers empty their purses for much stranger things. And so he saw green in her words. (And we don't mean lime Jell-O.)

Today little Sheri eats off the money her dad makes filling America's demand for anatomically correct molds of nonprivate body parts. In addition to the hands Sheri suggested, the El Segundo, California–based SKS Sibley Company now also makes molds for gelatin hearts, eyes, and brains.

The brain molds are by far its most popular product, and Halloween parties, by far the most popular occasion for its use, although Ken Sibley says he also gets a fair amount of business from biology teachers and hospital employees. One University of Southern California medical school brain researcher told him she decorates her gelatin brain dessert with cherry "brain tumors." (More common "enhancements" include axes and red food coloring.) At least one Christian illusionist uses the mold to teach Bible lessons. (Eric Reamer suggests sticking Bible verses on one side of the brain mold and gummy worms on the other to demonstrate what the Book of James says about a double-minded man being "unstable in all his ways.")

Sibley has only branched out from his human body part focus twice.

Once was to make a two-part gelatin mold of an alien so that people could re-create the alien autopsy performed on the 1995 Fox TV special of the same name. But he says, "It didn't take off." (And how could it, when the alien was dead and strapped to an operating table?)

An SKS Sibley gelatin mold depicting the face of Superior Court Judge Lance Ito was also part of the commercial circus that went on outside of the courtroom during the O. J.

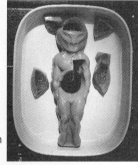

Simpson trial in 1995. Sibley said he created Eat-A-Ito to draw attention to his company and its other products but mainly it drew the attention of the Judge, who told him to cease and desist.

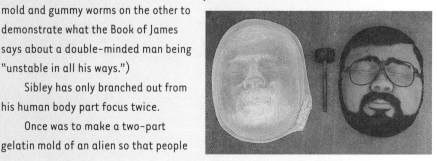

Emory University fraternity's tradition of flatbedding a 7-foot-by-7-foot-by-2-foot vat of Jell-O from the cafeteria to the rear of their fraternity house each October so that half-naked, blindfolded pledges-to-be could be led outside one by one and given the heave-ho into the Jell-O.

JELL-O Shots

College kids also created Jell-O shots, according to the Smithsonian's Jeff Brodie. Made with Jell-O and vodka or fruit-flavored liquor, Jell-O shots were the perfect alcoholic delivery system for new drinkers because the Jell-O masked the taste of alcohol and allowed the drinker to still think of herself as a child,

said Brodie during a talk entitled "A Short History on the Creation of Vodka Jell-O, or The Corruption of an American Childhood Institution" at the 1991 Smithsonian Jell-O conference. Jell-O also allowed for a much more even distribution of liquor than the vodka-injected oranges that get thrown from rented houseboat to rented houseboat during spring break on Lake Havasu in Arizona, said Brodie, who claimed to have done primary research.

Dessert of (Wrestling) Champions

That's not even the worst misuse of Jell-O. That would easily be Jell-O wrestling, invented in the early '80s as a less grimy alternative to mud wrestling. Red Jell-O does not sting the eyes like spaghetti sauce and pudding, and also allows for better body viewing than almost any other wrestling substance, Jell-O wrestler Spanish Rose told a reporter. "You're . . . a little red, but you can see the definition."

Rose was part of the Chicago Dolls team of bikini bathing-suit-clad wrestlers who appeared at the Rustic Lounge in suburban Chicago once a month in the early 1980s to wrestle in Jell-O. The Dolls themselves made the Jell-O, then dumped it on the wrestling mat by the bucketful in front of the yelping crowd.

Jell-O wrestling also made a six-year stand at Sam's Crab House restaurant in suburban Washington, D.C., a family restaurant where standing on an opponent or holding her head under the Jell-O was strictly forbidden, Ellen Hughes told her Smithsonian Jell-O conference audience in her talk, "Jell-O Wrestling: Tasteless Entertainment or Alternative Sport for Women?" Sam's Jell-O was really artificially colored unflavored gelatin to which Sam would occasionally add a dollop of whipped cream and a cherry, "for show."

Jell-O wrestling's quest for respectability suffered a setback in 1995 when National Football League officials read the riot act to some NFL players scheduled for appearances on a Florida gambling

cruise that also featured nude Jell-O wrestling (although the objection was to the gambling rather than the Jell-O).

This highly publicized cruise notwithstanding, the popularity of Jell-O wrestling as adult entertainment had largely died out by 1986, replaced by interest in the sport as a fund-raiser for high schools and AIDS organizations.

Prom queens, Camp Fire Girls, and leprechauns have all gone down for the count and a minimum of $100 in pledged donations at one of the oldest and largest of Jell-O AIDS fund-raisers, sponsored by the Southern Arizona AIDS Foundation in Tucson and hosted by four drag queens who have been known to auction off their clothes for the cause.

Advice columnist Ann Landers was asked to comment on Jell-O wrestling in 1987 by a reader who saw in it the reason for Americans' worldwide

reputation as "a mindless, hedonistic and nutty people." Landers declared it "disgusting" but better than illegal dog fights.

Jell-O wrestling is more often criticized for exploiting women. In 1986, University of Pittsburgh officials put a kibosh on a fraternity's plans to sponsor a Jell-O wrestling match between two women for just this reason—an action that prompted the local chapter of the American Civil Liberties Union to defend Jell-O wrestling as part of students' constitutionally guaranteed right of freedom of expression. (Really.)

And the controversy continues judging from this response to an editorial in a Purdue University school newspaper that questioned a February 2000 Jell-O wrestling event on campus. "How does wanting to have school spirit . . . and encouraging good wholesome fun make you ashamed of Purdue? It [Jell-O wrestling] is one of the few things you can do on a Friday night that doesn't include drinking and in which the participants are totally clothed . . . ," began the letter from Heather "The Incredible Edible Hulk" Steger, Amber "The Animal" Laffoon, Amy "Toxic Shock" Schultz, and one other Purdue coed.

JELL-O Fun-Raisers

Fortunately for those who would just as soon avoid Jell-O wrestling with the National Organization for Women, there is a Jell-O fund-raising alternative. It is the gelatin slide, splash, or jump. They're all different names for the same basic concept, which is to fill a swimming pool with Jell-O and get people to pay money (or get pledges) for the privilege of sliding in. Such events can raise upwards of twenty thousand dollars for the sponsoring charity, commonly leukemia societies, although it's far from easy money.

"It's not something you undertake lightly," said Joan Jarrett, executive director of the Gulf Coast Leukemia & Lymphoma Society in Houston, and the slide's founding mother. "There are logistics"—such as finding enough volunteers to open 4,800 little Jell-O boxes should grocery stores donate the gelatin. This is not to mention mixing and making sure it sets (a leukemia group once got sued by a woman who broke her ankle while sliding into what she claimed was "nothing more than colored water"), and protecting floors and spectators from flying gelatin. Yes, some of these events are held indoors—including, incredibly, in hotel ballrooms (let's hope the wedding party that gets the room next wears boots).

Still, "It's an easy event to sell because it's so unique," says Sheri Coombs of the Central Pennsylvania Chapter of the Leukemia & Lymphoma Society, now in its ninth year of gelatin moneymaking. Corporate participation is particularly strong, in part because, "People will ante up to send the boss down the slide," Coombs says.

And what's it *like* to slide into gelatin?

"It's gross," said Paul Gardner after making the plunge at the Indiana chapter of the Leukemia Society of America's fifth annual Gelatin Splash in 1997.

JELL-O Stunts

People will do even wackier things with Jell-O when they're the ones getting the cash or prizes. Letting people dive into a vat of gelatin to try to find money or keys to a new car is a common radio station promotion. Less common is one Michigan ski area's annual construction of a Jell-O pit for their spring Jell-O Jump (although most skiers fall in) and the Jell-O iMac contest held at the Massachusetts Institute of Technology in 1999. The latter challenged students to create the colorful computers out of the equally colorful Jell-O. The first-place winners mimicked the real thing down to its fish tank screensaver.

Sometimes the Jell-O stunts are individual efforts such as Steve Lugon's 1985 public bellyflop into a tub of Jell-O in San Francisco 49er colors for some tickets to see them play in the Super Bowl. Evan Hansen of Provo, Utah, earned $5,000 for cutting the roof off a station wagon and filling it with 1,000 pounds of raspberry Jell-O and 16 gallons of whipped cream in another radio station contest (although he only had $4,500 after paying the fine for unlawfully dumping the Jell-O into a storm drain).

Primal Powder

Jell-O is also loved by lovers—at least according to the "Sexy Edibles" section of a 1996 *Cosmopolitan* magazine article entitled "Tools for Love." And how could anything with as much wiggle-jiggle as Jell-O not have animal attraction?

Yes, that's right, love for Jell-O isn't even restricted to our own species. It's also popular with fruit bats at the Toronto Zoo, who fall for vitamin-fortified strawberry Jell-O as readily as human kids fall for Jell-O mold-disguised vegetables. And Jell-O is both food and plaything for primates at a number of American zoos and animal parks.

"The chimps like Jell-O just as much as we do," says L J Margolis of Florida's Lion Country Safari. Scientists looking for proof of chimp's kinship with man need look no further.

Little Mama and Nana enjoying Jell-O at Florida's Lion Country Safari

---

JELL-O as Plant Food, Hair Dye, and Foot Soak

Most people think of Jell-O as a food, and sure, Jell-O can make delicious salads and desserts. But it can also be a household helper with the versatility of baking soda.

Gelatin's most famous alternate use is as plant food. (Its protein is supposed to enrich nitrogen-poor soil.) The pleasant fruity smell and mild acids in Jell-O also make it an effective cleaner-freshener. Try putting a package or two of Sugar Free lemon Jell-O through the wash cycle of your dishwasher to get rid of soap buildup and hard water stains, or use it to scrub the shower instead of Clorox.

Jell-O is also a good odor eater, according to one woman who sprinkles it on cat litter and another who uses it as a foot soak. It made her feet smell so great that her husband took to licking them.

But by far the most popular nonculinary use for Jell-O involves hair care. Dissolve a box of Sugar Free lemon Jell-O in a quart of warm water to make a cheap setting lotion. (Although stiff at first, your hair should comb out silky, shiny, and tangle free.)

Methods vary for dying your hair bright colors with Jell-O. Some young punks simply dunk or paint their hair with Jell-O dissolved in hot water; others dissolve one or two boxes of Jell-O into a conditioner mixed with a few drops of water and work it through their wet hair. Whichever method you choose, use Sugar Free Jell-O, unless you want a halo of flies.

Jell-O is also used to dye wool and other natural fabrics. Although more expensive and less certain than other methods, Jell-O is good when working with children. "It attracts their attention and you won't lose anybody if someone decides to drink the dye pot," explains Eileen Hett, an Edmonton weaver whose Jell-O dying mix includes one small package of Jell-O, a half cup of vinegar, a teaspoon of salt, and a quart of water.

And if any Jell-O color should happen to stain your hands or countertops: real baking soda mixed with a bit of water is the universally recommended solution.

How to Make a **JELL-O** Wrestling Mat OR Fill a Pool for a **JELL-O** Slide:

S O M E   I N S T R U C T I O N S   F O R   D O - I T - Y O U R S E L F E R S

For the mat: Place some padding and a tarp inside an 8- to 10-foot square padded frame. To get the recommended 2- to 3-inch Jell-O mat, you'll need 55 to 70 gallons of Jell-O. Most people make it in 5-gallon buckets using anywhere from the same proportion of water as is recommended on the Jell-O box to up to twice as much (or anywhere from 8 to 16 small or 4 to 8 large boxes of Jell-O per bucket). All the usual rules about using boiling water and dissolving the Jell-O completely apply and are even more crucial given the quantities involved.

For a pool party people won't soon forget: About 600 to 700 gallons of Jell-O will be needed to fill an 8-foot-diameter pool. The Jell-O chef for the Central Pennsylvania Chapter of the Leukemia & Lymphoma Society's annual Gelatin Slide favors a thick Jell-O. He pours boiling or hot water to within 6 inches of the top of each of 25, 30-gallon trash cans along with 36 pounds of lemon Jell-O, then refrigerates until set (typically four or five days).

Note: Unless you work at a restaurant or live in cold climes and it's winter, secure a spot in a cafeteria or restaurant refrigerator *first*.

Outlaw JELL-O

It may be time for a public service campaign advising people to use Jell-O responsibly. At least that's what you'd have to conclude after seeing the number of times Jell-O shows up on the nation's police blotters.

The most infamous case is the so-called Jell-O Murder, in which a Massachusetts woman got life in prison for putting a lethal dose of LSD in her boyfriend's Jell-O in 1990.

In 1993, a Los Angeles man tried to defend himself against a drunk driving charge by claiming that he had become unwittingly intoxicated by eating three bowls of gelatin that had been covertly laced with vodka by a friend. But the jury rejected his so-called Jell-O Defense.

In 1994, a University of New Hampshire English professor was found guilty of sexual harassment and suspended from teaching for a year for several "offensive remarks," including this tortured simile involving Jell-O: "Belly dancing is like Jell-O on a plate, with a vibrator under the plate" (although it's possible the school trumped up the sexual harassment charges in order to stop this guy from teaching English composition).

Then there were the St. Petersburg, Florida–area school kids who in 1997 "played" at dealing drugs by cutting Jell-O with sugar and selling it as "happy powder" to fellow students at wildly inflated prices (thereby displaying the kind of marketing acumen that could land them all jobs at a big food company someday).

But the news is not all bad.

Jell-O has also saved lives.

It happened in Phoenix, Arizona, in December 1994 when a Catholic priest who got up in the middle of the night to go into the kitchen for his customary midnight strawberry Jell-O saw flames in an adjoining office and dialed 911—thus saving his own life and those of two other priests.

"Thank God for Jell-O," the Reverend Robert Skagen said afterward.

Joys of Weird JELL-O

This book could not hope to compete with the 2,187 Jell-O gelatin recipes currently in the Kraft Kitchens database. What we can offer you are a few of the most unusual Jell-O recipes: some long-ago company creations that Kraft would probably just as soon now forget and some consumer generated (such as this first dish, an award-winning Asian-style Jell-O entrée by Mary Jo Ahlin).

Sweet Raspberry Chicken

8 tablespoons butter

4 boneless, skinless chicken breasts

1 (24-ounce) can pineapple chunks, drained

1 green pepper, diced

1 small yellow onion, diced

1 (18-ounce) jar orange marmalade

1/4 cup soy sauce

1 (6-ounce) package raspberry Jell-O gelatin

Sliced or slivered almonds (optional)

Preheat oven to 350°. Grease a 9 x 13-inch glass casserole dish with 1 tablespoon of the butter. Place chicken breasts in dish. Cover with pineapple, pepper, and onion. Melt 7 tablespoons of the butter. Microwave uncovered marmalade jar on high for 15 to 30 seconds. In a bowl, mix butter, softened marmalade, soy sauce, and dry Jell-O powder. Pour ingredients over chicken. Bake 40 to 45 minutes, stirring occasionally. Let sit 5 minutes before sprinkling with almonds (if desired) and spooning over cooked rice. Serves 6 to 8.

Strawberry Pretzel Salad

2 cups pretzels

3/4 cup (1 1/2 sticks) salted butter

1 (8-ounce) package cream cheese, softened at room temperature

1/2 cup sugar

1 (8-ounce) container Cool Whip

1 (3-ounce) package strawberry Jell-O gelatin

1 (3-ounce) package raspberry Jell-O gelatin

2 cups boiling water

1 (16-ounce) package frozen strawberries, thawed

1 (8-ounce) can crushed pineapple with juice

Preheat oven to 400°. Crush the pretzels with a rolling pin. Melt the butter and mix with the pretzels. Spread in the bottom of a 9 x 13-inch pan or oven dish. Bake 7 minutes. Set aside to cool.

Beat together the softened cream cheese and sugar. Gradually fold in the Cool Whip. Spread on the crust so that it is totally covered. Place the pan in the refrigerator. Dissolve the contents of the 2 Jell-O boxes in 2 cups boiling water and stir in the strawberries and pineapple. Chill until slightly jelled (about 1 hour). Pour the Jell-O mixture over the cream cheese filling.

Return the pan to the refrigerator for several hours or until completely set. Serves 8.

Pastel Cookies

3 1/2 cups flour

1 teaspoon baking powder

1 1/2 cups (3 sticks) butter or margarine

1 cup sugar

1 (3-ounce) package Jell-O gelatin, any flavor

1 egg

1 teaspoon vanilla

Additional Jell-O gelatin, any flavor (for best results, use same flavor)

Preheat oven to 400°. Mix flour and baking powder in medium bowl. Beat butter in large bowl with electric mixer to soften. Gradually add sugar and 1 package gelatin, beating until light and fluffy. Beat in egg and vanilla. Gradually add flour mixture, beating well after each addition.

Shape dough into 1-inch balls. Place on ungreased cookie sheets. Flatten with bottom of glass. Sprinkle with additional gelatin.

Bake 10 to 12 minutes or until edges are lightly browned. Remove from cookie sheets. Cool on wire racks. Store in tightly covered container. Makes about 5 dozen.

Orange-Glazed Duck

4- or 5-pound oven-ready duck

Salt

Celery stalks

1 cup water

8 whole cloves

1 (3-ounce) package orange Jell-O gelatin

2/3 cup firmly packed brown sugar

1 teaspoon vinegar

Rub duck inside and out with salt. Pin skin at neck over back of duck. Place celery in body cavity; draw opening together with poultry pins and lace twine around pins. Prick thoroughly with a fork. Place breast side up on rack in a shallow pan. Insert meat thermometer in thigh muscle next to body. Roast in a slow oven (325°) 35 to 40 minutes per pound or to 185° on thermometer.

Meanwhile, bring water and cloves to a boil. Remove from heat; stir in gelatin and sugar until dissolved. Add vinegar. About 45 minutes before duck is finished roasting, baste duck with drippings from pan. Then pour 1/3-cup gelatin mixture over duck. Finish roasting, basting frequently with remaining gelatin. Serves 4.

Red Hot Salad

1 (3-ounce) package cherry Jell-O gelatin

1/4 cup Red Hots or Cinnamon Imperials candies

1 cup boiling water

2 cups sweetened applesauce

Add Jell-O and cinnamon candies to boiling water and stir until completely dissolved. Cool to room temperature. Add applesauce. Pour into 4-cup mold and chill until firm, about 4 hours. Serves 6.

JELL-O Guacamole

2 cloves garlic, finely chopped

1 small onion, chopped fine

2 medium avocados, peeled and pitted

1 large tomato, diced

1 teaspoon ground coriander

1 teaspoon chili powder

1/2 teaspoon salt

1 cup boiling water

1 (3-ounce) package lime Jell-O gelatin

Hot pepper sauce to taste

Combine all ingredients through salt and process in a food processor or mash until smooth. Dissolve Jell-O in boiling water and add to avocado mixture. Season with hot pepper sauce. Coat a 6-cup mold with oil. Pour mixture in and refrigerate a minimum of 2 hours. Unmold and serve with tortilla chips.

Dry JELL-O Salad

1 (16-ounce) container small curd cottage cheese

1 (6-ounce) package orange Jell-O gelatin

1 (8-ounce) container Cool Whip

1 (11-ounce) can mandarin oranges, drained

1 (8-ounce) can pineapple tidbits, drained

Combine all ingredients. Let set in refrigerator 1 hour. Serves 8.

JELL-O Drink

1 (3-ounce) package Jell-O gelatin, any flavor

1 cup hot water

3 cups cold water

Dissolve Jell-O completely in hot water. Stir in cold water. Drink immediately.

JELL-O Sorbet

3/4 cup boiling water

1 (3-ounce) package strawberry or raspberry Jell-O gelatin

1/2 cup sugar

2 cups cold fruit juice, any flavor

Stir boiling water into gelatin and sugar in large bowl at least 2 minutes until completely dissolved. Stir in cold juice. Pour into 9-inch square pan. Freeze 1 hour or until ice crystals form 1 inch around the edges. Spoon into blender container. Cover. Blend on high speed about 30 seconds or until smooth. Return to pan.

Freeze 6 hours or overnight. Scoop into dessert dishes. Store leftover sorbet in freezer. Serves 8.

Mock Strawberry Preserves

3 cups mashed figs (about 20 medium figs)

1 (6-ounce) package strawberry Jell-O gelatin

3 cups sugar

Mix figs, Jell-O, and sugar in a large saucepan. Bring to a boil over medium heat and boil 15 minutes, stirring occasionally. Pour quickly into hot, sterile jars and seal jars with hot paraffin wax. Fills 6 medium jars.

JELL-O Popcorn

1 (3-ounce) package Jell-O gelatin, any flavor (not sugar free)

1 cup sugar

1 cup Karo syrup

1 large bowl of popped popcorn

Place first three ingredients in a saucepan and cook over low heat until clear. Pour mixture over popcorn and stir. When cool enough, shape into balls.

JELL-O Fruit Soup

1 (3-ounce) package raspberry or mixed fruit Jell-O gelatin

Dash of salt

1 cup boiling water

1 (10-ounce) package frozen raspberries

1 tablespoon lemon juice

1 1/2 cups cold water

1/2 cup sour cream

Nutmeg

Dissolve gelatin and salt in boiling water. Add the frozen raspberries, stirring until berries separate. Stir in lemon juice and cold water. Chill 30 to 40 minutes. Season the sour cream with nutmeg to taste and serve on soup. Serves 6 to 8.

Barbecue JELL-O

1 (3-ounce) package lemon Jell-O gelatin

1 cup boiling water

1 cup your favorite barbecue sauce

Mixed salad greens

Grease an 8 x 8-inch square pan. Dissolve the Jell-O in the water, then let cool to room temperature. Add the barbecue sauce and pour into the pan. Chill until firm. Cut into cubes and serve on greens. Serves 6.

JELL-O Marzipan Candy

1 (7-ounce) package fine-grated coconut

1 (3-ounce) package Jell-O gelatin, any flavor

1 cup blanched almonds, grated

2/3 cup sweetened condensed milk

1 1/2 teaspoons sugar

1 teaspoon almond extract

Food coloring (optional)

Mix all ingredients thoroughly. Shape into small fruits, vegetables, hearts, or other forms. Use food coloring to paint details. Chill until dry. Store, covered at room temperature. Makes 2 to 3 dozen candies.

Acknowledgments

I write alone but without much help I would have little to write about. So, in addition to being a lot of work and fun, this book is a written testament to people's kindness and generosity. That generosity started with the executives at Kraft Foods, Inc., and Hunter Public Relations who entrusted their baby to me. I could not have written this book without the cooperation and help of Mary Jane Kinkade, Becky Haglund Tousey, Grace Leong, Nora Bertucci, and Camille Rustige; as well as the cooperation and assistance of Lynne Belluscio and her helper, Andrea Capwell.

Mary Jane made everything possible and "set up" many useful interviews. Nora and Camille fielded the bulk of my pesky questions. Becky and Lynne opened both their archives and their minds to me in ways that have helped this book beyond measure (or measuring cup!). As the director of the historical society in the town of Jell-O's birth, Lynne probably knows more about Jell-O's history than anyone on earth. I cannot recommend highly enough her own musings on our subject of mutual fascination, *The Jell-O Reader* (available through the Jell-O Gallery museum).

This book has also greatly benefited from a number of academic books and papers about Jell-O (yes, there have been some!), especially Rosemarie Bria's 1991 Columbia University Teachers College doctoral dissertation, "How Jell-O Molds Society and How Society Molds Jell-O," Diane Nelson's Iowa University study of Jell-O advertising in *Ladies' Home Journal*, and Laura Shapiro's *Perfection Salad*.

Current or former General Foods, Kraft, or Young & Rubicam employees Bob Lowe, Margery Schelling, Janet Myers, Connie Longshore, Dick Helstein, Dana Gioia, Roy Mahrenholz, Harold Gears, Alden Sharp, Lovina Wessell, Al Hampel, and John Ferrell provided invaluable insight and information from the front lines. I am also greatly indebted to Jell-O collector Marilyn Felling for research help, photographs, and the loan of her Jell-O wrestling tape; and to Colin Bryan, Bruce Poulterer, and others from Leiner Davis Gelatin and associated companies for insights about how gelatin is made and sold around the world.

Others who went above and beyond include Lindsey Jones, Paul Heckbert, Scott Perry, Mary Suggett, Peter Liebhold, Jeff Tinsley, Talley Dunn, Dick Johnson, members of the Woodward and Wait families (especially Martha Tabone), David Siegel Radio Archives (of Yorktown Heights, New York), Viola Wyman, Douglas Wyman, Philip Greenvall, Joyce Morral, Karen Evans, Marc Abrahams, Robert Greenway, Indra Stern, Tina Schrager, Diane McWhorter, Carol Bronstein, Sylvia King, Nancy Hubbard, Wanda Hartz, Barbara Shuckra, Jennifer Winter, Saviah Hillam, Joe Koza, Judy Belushi Pisano, the staff of the Russell Library, Lee Hebert, Jon Gardiner, Rod Richardson, Tom Ford, Ann Dallas, Zach Feuer of Lawrence/Feuer/Lamontagne Gallery in New York City, and Mara Lavitt (the last, for once again rising to the considerable author-photo challenge).

I'd also like to thank the Bee and Missionary Society of the First Church of Christ in Middletown, Connecticut, for creating a feast of their favorite Jell-O dishes and to photographer friend Melanie Stengel for taking such a beautiful picture of them.

If sampling those molds was a high point of my Jell-O research experience, then the low one was the two weeks when a box containing one-third of all the photos in this book appeared to be lost, and I was reduced to something very much like quivering Jell-O! I had had a taste of editor Kati Steele Hesford's considerable diplomatic and editorial skills while working on *Spam: A Biography* but the missing box crisis helped *me to appreciate her quiet confidence and cool unshakability. To Kati and assistant Nicole Coscarelli I give my thanks and my promise to use Federal Express from now on.*

Finally I'd like to thank publicity whiz Marissa Del Fierro; my husband, Phil Blumenkrantz, Mr. Congealiality; and my parents for raising me in a country crazy enough to love such an unusual food.

Illustration and Text Credits

Courtesy Kraft Foods, Inc. JELL-O, KNOX, COOL WHIP, CHEEZ WHIZ and all derived terms are trademarks of Kraft Foods Holdings, Inc., a subsidiary of Kraft Foods, Inc. and are used by permission: cover, title page, iv, v, vi, vii top and background, x left and right, xi, xiv, 1 left, top right, bottom right and background, 3 background, 5 right, 10 background, 12 right, 14 background, 15 bottom and recipe, 16 top right, bottom right and top left, 18, 19 top, 20 bottom and background, 21 background, 23 recipe, 25 top and bottom, 26 left and right, 28 top, 31 right, 32 background, 33 right, 35 right, 38, 39 left and background, 40 left background and song lyrics, 41 middle and background, 42 left and recipe, 43 song lyrics, 44 background, 46 recipe, 47 recipes, 48 right and background, 49 top, 50, 51 photo and recipe, 52 bottom, 54 all, 56 left and right, 57 top and bottom, 58, 59 top, bottom and background, 60 top and background, 61 (song lyric and ad), 62 top, middle, and background, 64 left and right, 65 top and bottom, bottom left, top left and background, 66, 67 top, 69 photo and recipe, 70 all, 71 background, 76 background, 79 all, 80 right background, 84 top and background, 86 recipe, 90-91, 96 recipe, 101 photo and poem, 102 background, 118 background, 122-123 background, 125 recipe, 126 right, 127 top right and middle right, 132-133 background, 134, 139 right recipe, 140 background left, background bottom and all recipes, 141 top right recipe and bottom right recipe, 142 background and all recipes.

LeRoy Historical Society, LeRoy, N.Y.: ix left and right, 2 bottom, 3 top and bottom, 4 top, middle, and bottom left, and middle and bottom right, 5 top left, 6, 8 left, 10 text, 14 top, 15 top, 16 bottom left, 22 left and right, 24, 27, 28 bottom, 32 left, 39 right, 43, 46, 48 left, 49 bottom, 52 top, 72, 73, 74 bottom and background, 75 top left and bottom left, 76 top and bottom, 79, 82 left, 83 top, 110 top, 124 bottom left, 128 top. Photos on 4 (bottom left), 28, 32, 82, 110 and 124 by Gennelle Thurman.

Viola M. Wyman: xii, 2 top (photo by Kristen Somody).
The Cooper Union for the Advancement of Science & Art: 2 bottom.

Author: 4 background (photo by Kristen Somody), 5 top right, 11 bottom left and bottom right, 12 left, 29 recipe, 75 recipe, 85 top (photo by Andrea Capwell), 111 recipe, 119 top left recipe, 121 recipe, 123 recipe 127 sidebar text,139 (photo by Kristen Somody), 141 top left recipe.
Gennelle Thurman: 8 right, 85 bottom, 86 background.
Martha Tabone: 9 photo and recipe.
Courtesy Genesee County Chamber of Commerce: 11 background, 12 background.
Grunts & Postures, Inc., Salt Lake City, Utah: 13, 124 top left.
Daughter of Gertrude Elizabeth (King) Muir: 17.
Lyons Memorial Library, College of the Ozarks: 19 bottom.
Statute of Liberty National Monument, National Park Service: 21.
Courtesy The Jel Sert Company, Chicago, Ill.: 32 right.
Courtesy Jack Benny Collection, American Heritage Center, University of Wyoming: 33 bottom, 37.
© Globe Photos, Inc. 2001: 30-31, 34, 35 left.
AP/World Wide Photos: 55 top.
National Archives: 55 bottom.
Andy Oakland: 53 top and recipe, 141 bottom left recipe.
Paul B. Hill with assistance from Ron Hoffmann: 53 photo.
"Money" copyright 1991 Dana Gioia. Reprinted from *The Gods of Winter* with the permission of Graywolf Press, Saint Paul, Minnesota: 63.
Serni Solidarios: 67 bottom.
Bambara, Salt Lake City, Utah: 68 top, middle and bottom (recipe by Scott Blackerby), 122 top right, 123 recipe.
© Jeffrey Allred, Deseret News: 122 bottom right.
Marilyn Felling: 71 right, 82 top, 81 background, 119 bottom left recipe and background, 129, 140 background right, 141 left and right background.
Leiner Davis Gelatin: 77 top, middle and bottom, 81 top and bottom, 82 bottom right, 83 background, 120 (photo by Kristen Somody).
Drawings from *Ralph Steadman's Jelly Book* courtesy Ralph Steadman and Scroll Press, New York, NY: 78 top and bottom.